MW00355564

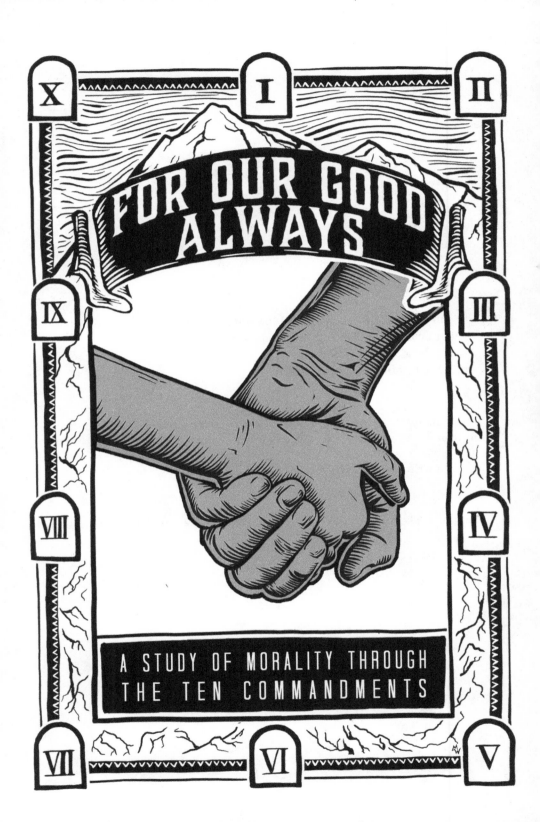

FOR OUR GOOD ALWAYS

A STUDY OF MORALITY THROUGH THE TEN COMMANDMENTS

For Our Good Always: A Study of Morality through the 10 Commandments:
© 2021 by Brandon Clements. All rights reserved.
Artwork by Matthew Wolfer
Published by Midtown Fellowship

All rights reserved. No part of this book may be reproduced or utilized in any form or by any means, electronic or mechanical, or by any information storage and retrieval system—except for brief quotations for the purpose of review, without written permission from the publisher.

Scripture taken from THE ENGLISH STANDARD VERSION. ©2001 by Crossway Bibles, a division of Good News Publishers.

TABLE OF CONTENTS

THINGS YOU NEED TO KNOW

BACKGROUND FOR THE BOOK

This book is written to be read in conjunction with a teaching series at Midtown Fellowship, a family of churches in the Columbia, SC metro area. You can find the sermons and additional resources for this series at ForOurGoodAlways.com.

This book is an attempt to answer important questions, such as:

- Who gets to decide between right and wrong?
- Do we each get our own truth?
- What does God say about morality?
- Why does God give us rules and boundaries?
- What is going on with some of the things I don't understand in the Bible?
- Why are some of my friends walking away from Jesus?
- Through history many people have rejected God because they wanted to act immorally...why does it seem like those walking away from God today believe God is the immoral one?

LAYOUT OF THE BOOK

The 13 chapters (listed on the left of the Table of Contents) will correspond with the sermons during this series. In the first 3 chapters, we will build some basic background knowledge and introduce something called "moral foundations," which are five different categories different cultures use to build their sense of right and wrong. (Don't worry, these will be explained later.) Then we will proceed to go through the Ten Commandments using those moral categories as lenses to help us understand them more fully.

In between each chapter is an interlude, which will contain additional content that will be helpful in building the overall argument for the book. Some interludes will be thorough, others will be shorter. They include important information for understanding the book as a whole, so skipping them may cause confusion.

Think of this as more of a study than a standalone book. It is not written necessarily for you to read through all at once, but to read the corresponding chapter and interlude during that week of the sermon series. (Ideally you'd read the chapter and the interlude in different sittings that week, but that's getting picky.)

SOME ADDITIONAL NOTES

- Hopefully this will be an insightful, challenging read, because it is intended to be. It is an ambitious project and attempts to tie a good many concepts together to form a cohesive whole. Certain ideas are woven throughout the book and will require your diligent attention.

  You may continue to wrestle with some of the concepts as you finish. That is okay, and even desired on our end. We want many things to land with unquestionable clarity. But an additional goal of this resource is to give you new language and categories to keep building on in the future. Our hope is that you will not close the ideas presented here when you shut the book, but continue to use them in years to come, as you make your own connections.

  We ask that you would not go into this thinking of it as a breezy read you can skim and get the meat out of, but one you may need to sit with and read slowly, or multiple times. It has some ideas that may take some marinating. Be sure to catch all of the sermons as well, because they will provide extra connective tissue.

- A few authors will be referenced significantly. One is Jonathan Haidt, a non-Christian professor and social psychologist whose research on morality greatly influenced this book. His work on moral foundations theory is profoundly insightful and helps explain so many things, even the political disagreements in our country (coming later to an Interlude near you). We believe these concepts are helpful enough that we will reference his work more often than we generally would for someone else in a resource like this. Others are Peter Leithart, whose beautiful little book on the Ten Commandments was a source for this book, and Kevin DeYoung, whose book was also helpful.

- Unless otherwise noted, all Scripture quotations are taken from the ESV.

- When talking about the "law" in the Old Testament, sometimes there is confusion over the different types of laws found there. Below is a quick summary to bring clarity.

THE 3 TYPES OF OLD TESTAMENT LAW

Moral Law—These laws concern boundaries foundational for humans living under God's rule, and apply to all people for all time. Think of the Ten Commandments as a good example of moral law.

Civil Law—These laws were for the theocratic nation of Israel in ancient times, and concerned how justice and governance would be administered in their nation. While there is much wisdom found in these laws, they do not apply to all people because we are not citizens of ancient Israel. For example, if someone stole your livestock, civil laws instructed what should be done.

Ceremonial Law—These laws directed the prescribed worship of God in ancient Israel, specifically the sacrificial systems to deal with the sins of God's people. These rituals are no longer binding for Christians, because Christ has sacrificed Himself once and for all and replaced the Old Covenant with the New Covenant of grace. Forgiveness occurs no longer through the blood of sacrificed livestock, but through repentance of sins and the blood of Jesus—the only perfect Son of God who stands in our place.

INTRODUCTION

WISHES & WORRIES

We have big hopes for this series, and we've been excited about it for a long time. We pray that God uses it to challenge and mature our thinking, to pull us out of the fish bowls we find ourselves in, and give us a profound vision of His character and nature that is bigger than any one culture's dominant vision of Him. We long for renewed minds that resist the strong tides of our culture, discerning spirits to spot half-truths that are difficult to see, and humbled hearts that see God as bigger and more beautiful than we ever imagined.

We pray for all those things and more, so that the God of Scripture will be lifted high as He so deserves, and so we will be formed into winsome missionaries reaching out to a confused culture in much need of some good news.

But we also have some concerns when approaching a series like this.

The year of our Lord 2021 is not only upon us, but is rapidly passing by at this point, with the many life changes brought by the coronavirus pandemic not many of us saw coming.

And while we rather disappointingly still don't have flying cars in 2021, we do have many other less thrilling things in abundance:

Rash judgments.

Political polarization.

Cynicism.

Distrust.

Oversimplifications.

And you can add on top of that radically different understandings of the world—what's right, what's wrong, how to define important words like: *good* and *evil*, *justice* and *injustice*, *progress* and *hope*.

The way books work is that they have to be written months in advance. (Weeks and months are needed to write, edit, rewrite, design, print, ship, etc.) In modern times, months feel like an eternity. Landscapes shift drastically in a few months. There's no way of telling what major events have happened since this was written.

All that to say, we are embarking on a challenging, stretching series during a season where almost everything is already heightened. Everything and everyone is ready to pounce on the things they don't like or agree with.

What better time to step in with a megaphone and say, "Actually—we're all wrong. About a lot of things."

There is a high likelihood that you will be offended about *something* during this series. There will be something you don't like or don't agree with. Something you struggle to consider due to previously held notions that you might not be able to even see in yourself.

Say it with me: *I will be offended during this series.*

Now say this: *And that's okay—it's good for me to be challenged.*

None of us dictate truth or reality. That's what this book is all about.

So we are asking all of us to approach this series with a mind open to challenging insight, a heart fully open to the loving authority of God, and a spirit that remembers our most important group membership is not imaged by a flag or political symbol or family crest, but a wooden cross cut from first-century trees in the Middle East.

We pray that the end result of this series would be a rugged confidence that the God who is enthroned above the heavens is for our good, always.

A BRIEF WORD ABOUT ELEPHANTS

NYU psychologist and researcher Jonathan Haidt has spent his career studying morality, and his work will be referenced significantly later in this book. Early in his writing career he wrote a book about happiness called *The Happiness Hypothesis*, in which he put forth a metaphor about why and how people make the decisions they do.

He said to picture an elephant with a rider on top of it. The elephant symbolizes the emotional side of human beings—the automatic, visceral reactions we have to things or ideas. The rider symbolizes the rational side of humans—the conscious, verbal, thinking side of our brains. Thus, oversimplified, the analogy is the Emotional Elephant and the Rational Rider.

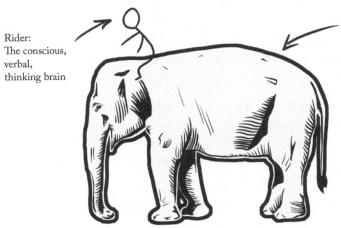

Rider:
The conscious,
verbal,
thinking brain

Elephant:
The automatic,
emotional,
visceral brain

Side note: If you are familiar with *Thinking, Fast and Slow* from Daniel Kahneman these are similar to his System 1 thinking (elephant) vs. System 2 thinking (rider).

The point of the analogy is to show that the way we judge things and make decisions doesn't happen the way we think it does. We think of ourselves, generally, as rational people that logically think through things with distance and clarity, then make a judgment. Once that decision has been reached by the Rational Rider who is in charge, the Emotional Elephant bows in submission and follows along with the direction.

Haidt's research shows that belief to be largely an illusion.

Rather, it's the quick, snap judgements the Emotional Elephant makes that lead the way. The elephant has a history, both personal and cultural, with countless stories and ideas hiding underneath the surface, and is predisposed to like certain ideas and dislike others. So often when presented with a judgment or decision, the elephant—what we might call our gut or intuition, or what research has shown to be subconscious bias—reacts before we even realize it. Automatically, based on evidence we aren't always cognitively aware of in the moment.

And when an elephant wants to go in a certain direction, what's a teeny little rider going to do to stop it?

Research suggests that what the rider often does is simply come up with the best logic possible to justify what the elephant has already decided. The rider still thinks he's in charge, but in reality, he's just concocting a post-hoc explanation. For example, if the person at your workplace you dislike the most gives a presentation, your Rational Rider may come up with reasons why the presentation lacked, but in all possibility the Emotional Elephant decided it wasn't going to like the presentation before any of those specific reasons existed.

While this is a helpful illustration, the Bible uses more timeless and theologically precise language for the same point. The Scriptures often talk about the heart as the driving motivation deep within us. Jeremiah 17 famously states that the human heart is deceitful and beyond our own understanding (Jeremiah 17:9).

Proverbs 3 instructs us on what to do with our hearts:

> *Trust in the Lord with all your heart,*
> *and do not lean on your own understanding.*
> *6 In all your ways acknowledge him,*
> *and he will make straight your paths.*
> *7 Be not wise in your own eyes;*
> *fear the Lord, and turn away from evil.*
> *8 It will be healing to your flesh*
> *and refreshment to your bones.*

> **Proverbs 3:5-8**

Proverbs 4 goes on to caution us to keep our hearts diligently, because "from it flows the springs of life" (Proverbs 4:23). Proverbs 14 cautions that "There is a way that *seems* right to a man, but its end is the way of death" (Proverbs 14:12, emphasis added). That "seems" is our gut, our elephant— making snap judgements almost instinctively. Our hearts steer and guide us through our affections and desires, but often end up on the path of death.

Whatever you want to call it, when encountering important, challenging ideas this is extremely important to keep in mind. There is a logical side of your mind, and you often think it is in charge, pulling the reins and directing that big old elephant—or your heart—where to go. That's understandable, because we all do.

It's also cute, largely false, and dangerous.

In reality, the elephant below is leading the way, reacting to things in ways you can't even see. The heart is leaning in ways that seem right to it. Deciding whether it likes something or doesn't and moving accordingly.

There will likely be ideas in this series, and most certainly as you encounter Scripture, that your elephant will have a strong negative reaction to. It will buck up, blow its snout in impassioned protest, and try to retreat.

We just need to know that this will happen. The things our elephants disagree with may to some degree have a common thread amongst humanity in general, but also have a wide variety between cultures and individuals.

So as we start this journey, we simply need to recognize and admit this. That we often "disagree" with things when in reality we just dislike them, and our dislike is covered in the language of argument. And while elephants are extremely powerful and persuasive—they are not always right.

"I don't like _____." does not = "_____ is not true."

As we move on, let's remember this. When we encounter things that don't seem right to us, that we don't like or agree with, let's stop and ask the Spirit if we are in line with truth and reality as He defines it.

Watch out for those elephants.

INTERLUDE 0
THE TEN NON-COMMANDMENTS & POST-CHRISTIAN CULTURE

Consider these opening lines from an article on CNN.com in 2017:

> *What if, instead of climbing Mount Sinai to receive the Ten Commandments from God, Moses had turned to the Israelites and asked: Hey, what do you guys think we should do?*
>
> *Considering the Hebrews' bad behavior in the Bible, what with the coveting of neighbors' wives and murdering their own brothers, that might have been a disastrous idea.*
>
> *But in our own more enlightened age, we're perfectly capable of crowdsourcing our own commandments — or, at least, that's what a new project would have us believe.*

The article, titled "Behold, Atheist's New Ten Commandments" went on to tell about a book written by Lex Bayer, an executive at AirBnB, and John Figdor, a humanist chaplain at Stanford University. Part of their project entailed crowd-sourcing the best list of ten "non-commandments" from thousands of willing atheist participants, seeking to prove that a consistent moral ethic can be crafted without belief in God.

The winning result of the contest was as follows:

1. Be open-minded and be willing to alter your beliefs with new evidence.

2. Strive to understand what is most likely to be true, not to believe what you wish to be true.

3. The scientific method is the most reliable way of understanding the natural world.

4. Every person has the right to control their body.

5. God is not necessary to be a good person or to live a full and meaningful life.

6. Be mindful of the consequences of all your actions and recognize that you must take responsibility for them.

7. Treat others as you would want them to treat you, and can reasonably expect them to want to be treated. Think about their perspective.

8. We have the responsibility to consider others, including future generations.

9. There is no one right way to live.

10. Leave the world a better place than you found it.[1]

There are many comments that could be made about this list, starting with the humorous idea of "non-commandments" in the first place. And well, #9 gives you reading whiplash, because heeding that one sure makes the others seem suspect...because the rest of the list sure does seem to be presented as the right way to live.

Pastor and author Kevin DeYoung, remarking on this study, notes the following:

> *"More to the point, these non-commandments are logically indefensible. They're presumably called "non-commandments" so as not to sound so commandment-ish. Yet they're all commands! They all carry the force of a moral ought. We live in a paradoxical age where many will say, "Right and wrong is what you decide for yourself," and yet these same people will rebuke others for violating any number of assumed commands. As a culture, we may be quite free and liberal when it comes to sex, but we can be absolutely fundamentalist when it comes to the moral claims of the sexual revolution. The old swear words may not scandalize us any longer, but now there are other words—offensive slurs and insults— that will quickly put someone out of polite company. We are still a society with a moral code."[2]*

---

1 "Behold, atheists' new Ten Commandments" www.cnn.com/2014/12/19/living/atheist-10-commandments
2 DeYoung, Kevin. *The Ten Commandments*. (Foundational Tools for Our Faith). Crossway. Kindle Edition.

Such is life in the modern, Western, secular world we live and move and have our being in. Our culture has a moral code indeed, and this list of non-commandments is at least a decent start to figuring out what it is. We live in a place and time that is absolutely allergic to the idea of commands, authority, dictates.

We are deeply suspicious of anyone or anything that claims hold over reality, even God, and the masses at this point are convinced that they each have their own individual "truth." As untenable, illogical, and asinine as that is, it holds little weight against the collective force of hundreds of millions of elephants—or deceived hearts—who all would very much like to get to determine what is true for them.

Because after all, there is no one right way to live, right?

The prevailing spirit of our age can be one of judgment upon the idea of commandments in the first place, and definitely the famous list given to us in Scripture. It is worth considering, however, why some would have such a revulsion to the actual list of Ten Commandments given to us.

Most of us are totally cool with a few of them: Don't murder...check. Don't steal...sounds great. Some of the others, however—we're not so high on as a culture. For example: forsaking idols, worshipping God alone, sexual restriction, Sabbath-keeping, and not coveting don't have quite the same curb appeal.

But for the non-commandment, live-your-truth crowd that surrounds us, it would be worth asking a hypothetical question. Let's say someone told you that your next door neighbor was going to break all 10 of the Ten Commandments in the next day.[3]

How would you feel? Are you nervous? Would you stay in your house or drive far, far away for the day?

On the flipside, what if someone offered you a place to live in a community where everyone at all times kept all ten?

Would that be appealing? Would part of you want to live there, seeing that you could give up your door locks and security system, never be lied to or

---

3 This exercise was posed in this video: www.tvcresources.net/resource-library/videos/
how-the-ten-commandments-inform-identity

about, never be defrauded or have a crime committed against you, and be surrounded by supremely content and respectful people?

Would the people that hate the idea of God's authority actually love its effects?

CONSIDERING THE CULTURE BEHIND NON-COMMANDMENTS

It's worth considering: what sort of culture was this incomplete and vague list of partly praise-worthy, partly confusing non-commandments birthed from? They were not pulled out of thin air, but crafted in a particular time and place.

One helpful breakdown sociologists have given to describe different types of cultures and their exposure to Christianity has been the following:

Pre-Christian Cultures: Pre-Christian cultures are those that existed before any influence from Christianity. Think about a people group in history who had no exposure to the teachings of Scripture, or a remote tribal village today. These groups have their own moral code and worldview developed without any contact with the Christian faith.

Thus, an encounter with the God of Scripture would be like an entirely new world breaking in, not totally dissimilar to what happened to the nation of Israel in the Old Testament when God gathered them to be His representatives and gave them the Ten Commandments and the rest of the law.

Christianized Cultures: Christianized cultures are profoundly shaped by Judeo-Christian values. It does not mean that every person is a Christian or that there aren't massive blind spots in the application of Scriptural teachings—but simply that Christianity is largely accepted, tolerated, and sometimes even celebrated as the ideal. Being a Christian in this context gains you social capital (which can lead to issues of its own).

1950s America is often a picture brought up to illustrate this type of culture. It is a good example of a Christianized culture, not because it is some bygone ideal we should strive for. There were significant failures here no faithful Christian would want to emulate, starting with rampant racism and discrimination at the top of the list.

A Christianized culture can be full of hypocrisy and void of spiritual vitality. This term simply means that in general, embracing Christian principles and morals is common, respected, and often comes with social acceptance.

Post-Christian Cultures: Post-Christian cultures that have been shaped profoundly by Christian beliefs and values, but have largely tried to move on from them. Historic Christian beliefs are tolerated to varying degrees socially, but increasingly are seen as antiquated. Embarrassing at best— oppressive and harmful at worst.

A post-Christian culture would be a place where a list of ten non-commandments such as the one above would promote general head-nodding by many. Because this culture would claim that we've moved on from ancient morals and ideas into more mature, enlightened thinking.

The ironic thing is, people in these cultures often don't realize how much they have benefited from the outdated codes that helped create the strengths of their society in the first place. Christian beliefs about humans being made in the image of God have driven much progress in human rights, dignity, and justice. Without those assumed, you can't have a post-Christian culture.

Examples of this kind of culture would include modern France, England, and increasingly the United States. Wherever the Enlightenment and Western Civilization has spread, you will find this on its heels. Though the heights of post-Christian culture tend to align with large coastal cities—its advance elsewhere has sped rapidly through modern media, the internet, and the smartphone. As people increasingly access the same information and hear the same stories through movies, TV and Netflix, the monoculture secular thought patterns of post-Christianity spread.

This is not all bad. Ask someone who grew up in the teeth of the Bible Belt, and they will tell you it's quite confusing when everyone calls themselves a Christian but hardly anyone's life looks like the picture of a Christian's life found in Scripture. It can bring clarity and simplicity when people know exactly where they stand spiritually, and you don't have to first convince someone that they actually aren't a Christian before you can explain how to become one.

In a post-Christian culture, when someone claims single-minded devotion to the teachings of Jesus and places themselves under the authority of the

Bible, they mean it. Because they sure aren't gaining anything socially from doing that. More likely, it's probably costing them respect or affirmation to one degree or another with their family, friends, or in their career.

Your experience may vary from others in our church, and it may have changed as you've grown older. We have members with varying backgrounds who would have differing opinions on where we fall on this scale. But on a macro-level, there is a sea change happening through the decades that surround us, and we are by no means unaffected by it.

There are benefits to this, and also challenges. Lord-willing, this book will help us think about some of those changes well and be equipped for them.

CHAPTER 1
FOR OUR GOOD, ALWAYS

THE ELEPHANT IN THE GARDEN

The oldest lie in the book, quite literally, is that God is not for our good.

Our first parents lived in a perfect world, unruined by sin, when the enemy came to tell them something insidious and deceitful. The serpent told them God was not to be trusted, that He did not have their best interest in mind and only wanted to keep them below Him. The deceiver's lie: "God knows that if you eat of the forbidden tree you'll be powerful like Him, and He doesn't want that." (Genesis 3:1-7)

That lie sounded awfully good to their elephants—their emotional, visceral selves—so they ate. When God approached them later, it was their rational rider that came up with justifications and explanations, but the reality was: they wanted to be God.

It was a revolt.

And the forbidden tree, it had a name. A purpose not to be overlooked. It was not a randomly selected tree that God chose just to see if they would trust Him—it was a very specific tree.

The tree of the knowledge of good and evil.

It was an intentional choice, because not eating from that tree meant they were accepting that God was wiser than them, that He got to determine what was good and evil, right and wrong. That He was God, and they were not. Eating of the tree meant "No—*I* get to determine what is good and evil."[4]

That was the heart of the matter. It was a rebellion, yes—but a rebellion about who got to decide what was right and wrong, who got to be God. The redefinition of good and evil was at the center of the act of rebellion.

And it still is.

---

4 Genesis 3:6

The redefinition of good and evil continues to play out today, and is at the heart of much of what we will discuss in this series. Pick any contentious issue and at the core of the argument you will find the question, "Who gets to say what is right and wrong—God, or us?" This is not new; it's very, very old.

We have always been prone to do whatever is right *in our own eyes*.

> *In those days there was no king in Israel. Everyone did what was right in his own eyes.*

> **Judges 21:25**

Throughout Scripture God makes the argument that He alone is the arbiter of reality.

That He alone is wise enough to discern good from evil.

That He has our best interest in mind, and is the only source of lasting joy for the human soul and flourishing for human society. The directive to avoid that tree was not arbitrary, but for our good.

And ever since the Garden, the consistent refrain has been that humans hear that and say, "Nah..."

THE ROAD TO THE TEN COMMANDMENTS

Things got dark very quickly after Adam & Eve chose to redefine good and evil. Rival gods were not welcomed in God's paradise, so they were removed. They worked the cursed ground and gave birth through hard labor. Two sons, Cain and Abel, approached God to give sacrifices, and Cain's sacrifice was not pleasing to the Lord. He grew jealous of his brother Abel, whose sacrifice was pleasing to God, and God came to him with a warning:

> *So Cain was very angry, and his face fell. 6 The Lord said to Cain, "Why are you angry, and why has your face fallen? 7 If you do well, will you not be accepted? And if you do not do well, sin is crouching at the door. Its desire is contrary to you, but you must rule over it."*

> **Genesis 4:5-7**

The revolt that started with his parents had now passed to Cain. He was angry that God did not affirm his sacrifice, and jealous of his brother. While we don't know details about their sacrifices, we can see that Cain was not happy about the terms on which acceptable sacrifices were decided. It enraged him that *God* got to decide what was acceptable and pleasing—that *God* set the terms for what made a desirable sacrifice.

God tells Cain that sin—the spirit and act of rebellion—is crouching at his door, with a desire to overtake him. And, it does. Cain's jealousy and outrage at both God and Abel lead him to commit the first murder in human history. A lesson that bad things ensue when we dictate the terms of what God should or should not accept, affirm, and allow.

This tragedy blossoms to a larger scale, as two chapters later God remarks that people on the Earth had become so hostile toward Him and each other that "every intention of the thoughts of his heart was only evil continually. And the Lord regretted that he had made man on the earth, and it grieved him to his heart" (Genesis 6:5-6).

God blots out the spreading wickedness ruining His creation through the flood, thereby cleansing the Earth and starting over with one family who found favor in God's sight. Noah's family repopulates the Earth, and in Genesis 12 God goes to a man named Abram and tells him that He is going to make his family a great nation and bless the whole world through his descendants. This was the start of the nation of Israel, who were to be God's priests and representatives, a covenant people to show the world what it is like to live under God's good reign.

But the theme of rebellion continues, because sin continues to crouch at their doors. They continue to take control over deciding what is good and what is evil, letting their elephants—or sinful hearts—lead the way. Demanding that their lives be lived on their terms and not God's. This ends with them being brutally enslaved in Egypt, crying out for God to rescue them. Which is exactly what He does, through plagues and wonders, defeating the kingdom of Pharaoh who had challenged the God of Israel at every turn.

God leads His people miraculously through the dry bottom of the Red Sea, into the wilderness, and into an existence where He would begin to reform and retrain them on what it is like to live life under God's authority.

This culminates on Mt. Sinai, as God gives the Ten Commandments, which are basic laws for approaching life as if God is in charge and He alone gets to decide what is right and wrong. These commandments were an act of re-submission to God's rule. Everything had gone wrong as a result of rejecting His authority, and His intent was to create a people who learned how to respect, honor, and obey Him.

ISRAEL AS RECLAIMED SON

Theologian Peter Leithart, in his book *The Ten Commandments: A Guide to the Perfect Law of Liberty* argues that there is a relational dynamic to the exchange of the Ten Commandments that we are in danger of missing. He notes that God speaks the commandments to all Israel, but uses the masculine singular "you" pronoun to address the commands, thus speaking to Israel collectively as His son.

> *"We may ask, Who was delivered from the house of bondage? Israel, of course, but Israel as son of Yahweh (see Exod 4:23). Yahweh's 'family' tie to Israel provides a legal basis for his demand to Pharaoh: 'Israel is my son. You have no right to enslave my son. Let my son go.' When Pharaoh refuses, Yahweh cuts off negotiations and takes up the role of a kinsman redeemer, rescuing his son with a mighty hand and outstretched arm. Yahweh's justice is precise: Pharaoh seized Yahweh's firstborn; at Passover, Yahweh takes Pharaoh's."*[5]

This brings an important angle to the ancient story you may have heard countless times. God is not some impersonal ruler looking for underlings to boss around, but a Father looking out for a prodigal son, aiming to rescue him from the mud pits of rebellion he'd run headlong into. God is an adopting, rescuing, redeeming God who intends to have a son who learns to trust Him and look like Him. He goes on:

"God gave his first command to Adam, his first son. At Sinai, he speaks to his son, the new Adam. The Ten Words are imperatives, but not merely imperatives. When Father Yahweh speaks to son Israel, he discloses his likes and dislikes. The Ten Words are 'a personal declaration' that reveals Yahweh's character. Like Proverbs, they're a Father-son talk. The ten new-creative words are designed to form Israel into an image of his Father."

---

5 | Peter Leithart, *The Ten Commandments.*

In redemptive history, Israel would prove unable to be such a son formed into the image of his Father. That much is made clear in time, and the good news of history is that God does have such a Son, blameless in every way and able to truly and finally rescue us from spiritual slavery.

But the Old Covenant God that instituted with Israel, though insufficient, is breathtaking. The Father cared so deeply about his wayward children that He sought them out in power, overthrew their towering oppressors, brought them back home and gathered them around the fire to teach them what it is like to live in His house, as His sons and daughters.

> *To you it was shown, that you might know that the Lord is God; there is no other besides him.* ₃₆ *Out of heaven he let you hear his voice, that he might discipline you. And on earth he let you see his great fire, and you heard his words out of the midst of the fire.*

Deuteronomy 4:35-36

These commands are notoriously famous and history-altering. They form the basis of historic Judeo-Chirstian morality, and arguably the bedrock of human thought about law. They also reveal the depths of the fatherly heart of God. He wants His adopted, redeemed kids to love Him and worship Him, so they will not be destroyed by the evil around them or the evil inside them.

Here are the family rules, as enumerated in Exodus 20:1-6:

> *And God spoke all these words, saying,*
>
> ₂ *"I am the Lord your God, who brought you out of the land of Egypt, out of the house of slavery.*
>
> ₃ *"You shall have no other gods before me.*
>
> ₄ *"You shall not make for yourself a carved image, or any likeness of anything that is in heaven above, or that is in the earth beneath, or that is in the water under the earth.* ₅ *You shall not bow down to them or serve them, for I the Lord your God am a jealous God, visiting the iniquity of the fathers on the children to the third and the fourth generation of those who hate me,* ₆ *but showing steadfast love to thousands of those who love me and keep my commandments.*
>
> ₇ *"You shall not take the name of the Lord your God in vain, for the Lord will not hold him guiltless who takes his name in vain.*

8 "Remember the Sabbath day, to keep it holy. 9 Six days you shall labor, and do all your work, 10 but the seventh day is a Sabbath to the Lord your God. On it you shall not do any work, you, or your son, or your daughter, your male servant, or your female servant, or your livestock, or the sojourner who is within your gates. 11 For in six days the Lord made heaven and earth, the sea, and all that is in them, and rested on the seventh day. Therefore the Lord blessed the Sabbath day and made it holy.

12 "Honor your father and your mother, that your days may be long in the land that the Lord your God is giving you.

13 "You shall not murder.

14 "You shall not commit adultery.

15 "You shall not steal.

16 "You shall not bear false witness against your neighbor.

17 "You shall not covet your neighbor's house; you shall not covet your neighbor's wife, or his male servant, or his female servant, or his ox, or his donkey, or anything that is your neighbor's."

THE "WHY" BEHIND THE TEN COMMANDMENTS (AND ALL OF GOD'S LAWS)

The Ten Commandments are repeated in the book of Deuteronomy, as Moses is preparing the Israelites for his death and reminding them of all that God had spoken to them. Amid this recounting, there is a beautiful section where Moses anticipates pushback and confusion that might come to God's laws for His covenant people.

As a family of churches, one of our leadership values is "Narrate it," which simply means when we lead, we need to tell others *what* we are doing, *why* we are doing it, and *why it is the best thing* for them.

This is exactly what Moses does in this passage—he narrates the law and the Ten Commandments.

20 "When your son asks you in time to come, 'What is the meaning of the testimonies and the statutes and the rules that the Lord our God has commanded you?'

In other words: one day, after some time has passed, it is likely that your children or their children won't understand the meaning and purpose for all that God has instructed us to do and not do. They will ask you, "Why did God give us this rule or that law?" His answer is glorious:

> ₂₁ *then you shall say to your son, 'We were Pharaoh's slaves in Egypt. And the Lord brought us out of Egypt with a mighty hand.* ₂₂ *And the Lord showed signs and wonders, great and grievous, against Egypt and against Pharaoh and all his household, before our eyes.*

First and foremost, because God saved us—He delivered us from slavery when we had no hope of saving ourselves. He redeemed us from miserable slavery and overthrew the most powerful ruler we'd ever seen.

> ₂₃ *And he brought us out from there, that he might bring us in and give us the land that he swore to give to our fathers.*

He did all of this because He is faithful. He keeps his promises. He said He was leading us to a good land, and He intended to do just that, because He is trustworthy.

> ₂₄ *And the Lord commanded us to do all these statutes, to fear the Lord our God, for our good always, that he might preserve us alive, as we are this day.* ₂₅ *And it will be righteousness for us, if we are careful to do all this commandment before the Lord our God, as he has commanded us.'*

> **Deuteronomy 6:20-25**

For our good. Always.

That's why He gave us the Law. To preserve us alive, as His sons and daughters, to keep us from harming ourselves and each other. He wants us to have a healthy fear of Him and respect for His authority. *"And it will be righteousness for us,"* as Moses says. All will be right and good and whole with us, if we are careful to obey Him as He has commanded us.

These words are a refutation of the original lie from the Garden—that God is not for our good and should not be trusted. Moses wants this to be ringing in the ears of God's people through generations and ages, from Sinai to Columbia.

He is for our good.

For *our* good.

For *my* good, for *your* good.

He is *for us*.

He can be trusted.

Always.

WE ARE THAT KID

When Moses writes, "When your son asks you in time to come," that downline includes us. We are the son, we are the daughter. We read and hear all of the guidelines and guardrails of God's law in Scripture, and some of them seem like common sense. Other commands, however, are diametrically opposed to what our culture says and can be confusing or conflicting.

So we, like the ancient Israelite child, ask, why? What is the meaning of these statutes and commands? Is God good if this is what He commands? Is He trustworthy?

The answer is the same for us:

We were slaves to sin, by nature children of wrath and under the reign of the devil, the "ruler of this world." And God saved us with His mighty, outstretched hand. The life, death, and resurrection of Jesus, the perfect Son, was a display of signs and wonders, great and grievous, that made a way for us to be rescued from slavery to sin, to ourselves, to Satan himself— and God brought us out of the kingdom of darkness into the kingdom of His beloved Son.

He brought us out of captivity, because He promised to do so long, long ago, and He is faithful and keeps His promises. He told the serpent in the Garden He was going to send a redeemer to crush his head, and He did (Gen 3:15).

So all that God commands of us, whether we understand it or not, is because He is for our good, always. Forever and ever and always. That He might preserve us in safety from all enemies inside and out. So that we will flourish, and all will be right with us when we submit to His authority.

This series—this book, is about us learning to trust that this is true. About learning how to be the sons and daughters God created us to be, and that God truly is, definitively and throughout all of history, for our good.

INTERLUDE 1
A WORKING THEOLOGY OF CONSCIENCE

There is a reason why we all have deeply held notions about what is right and wrong: God created us to do so.

We are moral beings. And by that, I don't mean "we have good morals," but rather that we have an innate sense and wiring that deals with the concept of morality. We have an inner judge that has strong inclinations about right and wrong, good and evil, justice and injustice.

Biblically, this is called our conscience. We read about it in Romans 2:14-16:

> For when Gentiles, who do not have the law, by nature do what the law requires, they are a law to themselves, even though they do not have the law. ₁₅ They show that the work of the law is written on their hearts, while their conscience also bears witness, and their conflicting thoughts accuse or even excuse them ₁₆ on that day when, according to my gospel, God judges the secrets of men by Christ Jesus.
>
> **Romans 2:14-16**

1. You Have a Conscience

The "law" is written on our hearts in such a deep way that our conscience bears witness to it. Our own thoughts can accuse us of wrongdoing like a prosecuting attorney questioning a guilty defendant. When this happens, even in people who don't have access to God's laws in Scripture, it provides evidence of the fact that God created us in His image.

This speaks to the guilt children sometimes feel over wrongdoing even before they understand the exact nature of their acts. When you were little, and you realized that it was kind of fun to pick on other kids at school, but it also made you feel bad when you saw the hurt on their face—that's your conscience.

We have onboard morality detectors. This is an important part of how God made you. It doesn't always keep you from doing what's wrong, because again—your heart is not pure, it's deceitful. It has warring desires and is good at justifying what it wants even if it's wrong.

But your conscience is always there functioning to some degree. It doesn't determine what is right and wrong, but it serves as a warning system. It helps explain the guilt you feel when you do something wrong and the outrage you feel when others sin in harmful ways.

2. Your Conscience Comes from God

Part of being created in His image is having his perfect law "written on our hearts" (Romans 2:15). This goes back to the design in the Garden of Eden. Our first parents were created to be the highlight of creation, special among all other creatures. An aardvark was not to be concerned with right and wrong, but Adam was—due to the elevated calling of being a co-ruler with God over the world.

Though elevated, we are not God. Co-ruling image bearers were designed to have *awareness* of what is good and what is evil, but not *control* over what is good and what is evil.

3. Your Conscience is Marred by Your Sin Nature

God created image-bearing reflections of Him with real agency that would submit to and resound the beautiful laws of reality, as defined by Him. But we did not submit our consciences to His authority. Instead, we used them to judge Him as unjust. In the Garden, Satan, and then Adam & Eve assigned God the role of oppressor. They used the gifts God had given them to declare freedom from Him.

They redefined good and evil, and we've been following in their footsteps ever since.

So your conscience is greatly marred by your sin nature. It's like a metal detector that fell out of a truck going down the highway—it's all bent and misaligned now. It still beeps sometimes when you put it near metal. But sometimes it doesn't. And sometimes it starts beeping when there is nothing metal nearby at all.

One way to think about this is that your conscience is affected by your "elephant," or your sinful heart. Your deceived heart has strong opinions about what you *want* to be good or what you *want* to be evil, and those desires easily get rationalized and co-opted into the language of conscience.

This broken conscience, especially when shaped by culture and lies, is why you can say or think things like, *"I know that God says it's wrong, but I don't feel conviction for it at all."* That doesn't mean God is wrong. That's because your conscience is broken by sin!

On the other side, your conscience could accuse you of things that actually aren't sinful from a biblical perspective. Our consciences are broken. We need help and clarity from the Holy Spirit.

4. Your Conscience is Shaped by Your Culture

More is coming on this, but sin is not the only thing that affects your conscience. The specific culture you find yourself born into also has a profound effect on how you are trained to think about right and wrong. So the "broken metal detector" of the USA will look different from the "broken metal detector" of Russia or Thailand.

This is why different letters to the churches in the New Testament often have different particular corrections. Because that group has gotten off track in a particular way. In the Old Testament, this is how entire nations spin off into total wickedness.

There are certain areas of your conscience that have been shaped by your culture and the people around you and you may not even know it. So there is a category for something that is so normative in your culture that it feels like "There's no way this is sinful," where you could actually be mistaken. You were just so desensitized to it that you couldn't see it.

Every culture has its own unique blind spots.

This is made clear by the reality that the things in the Bible we find difficult are not at all universal to humankind. Our culture in particular has a very hard time with God's wrath—His judgment on those who rebel against Him. We tend to think, through the lens of our collective consciences, "How is that okay? Isn't that harsh?" But if we were missionaries in some parts of the Middle East right now, those people would have absolutely no problem with the things we tend to find difficult.

They would have a problem with unearned grace. They would have a much harder time with the unmerited love and favor of God on sinful people, with a reaction more along the lines of, "Wait a minute...God forgives people? When they haven't done anything to earn it? No way...I can't accept that." You could craft what you consider is your most compelling argument for Christianity, and it may be the one they have the hardest time with. The surprising truth is that you would likely think about the world very differently if you would have been born into a different culture or time than ours.

5. Your Conscience Can be Seared

There is a scary warning in 1 Timothy 4:1-2:

> *Now the Spirit expressly says that in later times some will depart from the faith by devoting themselves to deceitful spirits and teachings of demons, through the insincerity of liars whose consciences are seared,*

> **1 Timothy 4:1-2**

Paul says the consciences of the false teachers have been seared (that is, desensitized and rendered ineffective) by their rebellion against God. Deceitful ideas that stem from Satan, and trust in those ideas, can lead a person or group's conscience to be scarred and hardened like a burnt steak, leaving them unable to recognize that what they think is good is actually evil in disguise.

The classic example, from a societal perspective, is Adolf Hitler's Nazi regime less than a century ago. Germany at that time was a leading force in Western civilization, and somehow descended into a belief system that advocated the best thing for their country was the extermination of an entire race of people. And somehow they reconciled that with their conscience.

(Let that sink in for a second.)

They weren't like, "We know this is pure evil, but who cares?" They reasoned themselves there. Their broken consciences, surrounded by unique circumstances and forces in their culture, led them like a carrot on a stick and they followed.

Going further back in history, our forefathers somehow came to the conclusion that it was justifiable to kidnap millions of people from Africa and bring them over here to forcefully enslave and build our new country. Those acts were justified by sinful, seared consciences deadened to the voice of God.

In the Old Testament, God's people were constantly warned not to adapt the corrupt and unthinkable beliefs and practices of nations around them. One such belief and practice came in the form of worship for the Ammonite god, Molech (Leviticus 18:21). Worshippers, believing that sacrificing to Molech would gain them a better life, would approach a giant animal-headed statue with a ravenous fire in its belly, and place their first-born child into the fire of its altar.

They practiced barbaric child-sacrifice, not because they were consciously operating out of evil intent, but because their shattered and seared consciences led them to that grotesque conclusion.

Just to be clear, all of this should be terrifying. We would be foolish to think the same thing couldn't happen to us, as if our consciences are in less danger of being seared corporately or individually. It's very difficult to see the cracks in your own culture's collective conscience.

We all face the same historic temptation to call good evil and evil good.

CHAPTER 2
GOD'S MORALS ARE DIFFERENT THAN YOURS

"You shall not do according to all that we are doing here today, everyone doing whatever is right in his own eyes..."

Deuteronomy 12:8

UNCOVERING ROMANS 2 IN RESEARCH

Jonathan Haidt, the previously mentioned social psychologist and author, has dedicated his career to the study of morality. He became fascinated with the way different cultures and times come up with their moral codes, and the culmination of his study is a book called *The Righteous Mind: Why Good People are Divided by Politics and Religion.*

In a podcast with a conservative media personality, he explained that he grew up Jewish in New York, and started his research, in his own words, "to help Democrats win elections."[6] He sensed decades ago that Democrats were losing elections, in part, because Republicans were able to connect with voters on more underlying categories of morality.

As time went on he became more centrist, not wanting political agendas to get in the way of his very insightful research—research that actually explains our political divisions in the first place (more on that later). *The Righteous Mind*, a suggested resource for this series, is packed full of brilliant human and cultural observations, but we believe Haidt's research only uncovered what Romans 2 already told us: that God has written His laws on the human heart.

Haidt's main thesis is that humans come hard-wired with moral intuitions, and that there are several different categories of morality that function almost like taste buds. He covers 5 different foundations for morality:

---

6 Sunday Special, Episode 22: Jonathan Haidt by the Ben Shapiro Show https://soundcloud.com/benshapiroshow/sundayspecialep22

CARE/HARM	This foundation is exactly what it sounds like. It's protecting individuals from being harmed. It wants to prevent pain. The virtues of this foundation are kindness, gentleness, and compassion. The greatest sins are being cruel, harsh, or insensitive. We know that something is wrong because you are harming others. Others are victims of your actions or inactions.
FAIRNESS/ CHEATING	This foundation is concerned with people being treated fairly. It is about justice, rights, and autonomy. The greatest sins here are cheating, deception, and injustice. It goes from racial or ethnic groups getting trampled on, to infidelity in marriage, to a kid taking a toy away from another kid, to you beating a vending machine that took your dollar.
LOYALTY/ BETRAYAL	The next two get more communal in nature. Loyalty is about the necessity in life to form cohesive coalitions to accomplish a goal, and the necessity of humans to group up in order to flourish. This leads to patriotism, group pride, and individuals being willing to self-sacrifice for the good of the group. The greatest sin here is to be a traitor or to be disloyal.
AUTHORITY/ SUBVERSION 	Also more communal in nature, It emphasizes the need for us to forge beneficial relationships within hierarchies, and insists that not all hierarchies are evil or exploitative. Respect for legitimate authority, whether it be God, a parent, boss, government, etc. leads to a general respect for traditions and a deference to those above you. The greatest sin here is disrespect or blatant disobedience.
SANCTITY/ DEGRADATION	This foundation claims that some things are right and wrong simply because God says they are. There is a vertical axis where some things are elevated, holy, set apart, sanctified...and below some things are evil, degrading and contaminating. The greatest sin here is defilement from doing something evil or degraded.[7]

7 Later in the book he adds a 6th category, Liberty/Oppression, teasing this out of the Fairness category, but for the sake of simplicity in this book we'll stick with the original five.

These categories, he argues, form the baseline instincts and judgments that different cultures use to construct their own morality. For example, Asian cultures tend to be far more communal and group-oriented in nature than Western culture. So if we were to map out generalized pictures of their culture, their marks for Loyalty and Authority would be far higher than a typical American graph would be. These cultures tend to see themselves as having much greater responsibility for each other than we do in Western cultures.

Likewise, Middle Eastern countries where Islam is predominant would likely see the apex of their graph on Sanctity. There is a praiseworthy emphasis of moral purity and religious observance through Middle Eastern cultures that actually explains the negative extremes. Part of the reason Middle Eastern Extremists are motivated to commit terrorist attacks is because they believe Western culture is bad for the world, polluting the Earth with gratuitous sexualization and "anything goes" morals. So they want to rid the world of these evils.

Now, where would our Western culture skew if we were graphed out, most likely? We would lean heavily towards care/harm, with a similarly dosed heaping of fairness for good measure.[8] Westerners tend to care deeply about protecting individuals from harm, and ensuring that people are treated fairly, and those are beautiful motives. For us, these categories tend to be heavily prioritized. There is a lot more nuance to bring once you get down into differences among us as a particular culture, but painting in the broadest strokes in comparison to other cultures and times, we lean hard in that direction.

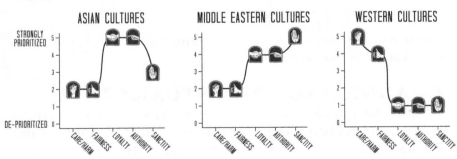

Disclaimer: These are generic graphs we created simply to illustrate priorities in different cultures and are not meant to be exhaustive descriptions.

---

8 This is a conclusion Haidt discusses in chapter 5 of *The Righteous Mind*.

Let's prove it. Finish the sentence below. You can do it without even thinking hard:

Do whatever you want, as long as it doesn't _____ someone.[9]

Did you even hesitate for a second answering? Of course you didn't.

One more proof, just for good measure. In the last few decades as technology began to advance dramatically, piracy became a massive problem. From Napster (remember that, anyone over 30?) to torrents, our culture had to come up with a way to try to convince people that stealing was wrong.

What did the powers that be in our culture come up with?

Piracy is not a _____ crime.[10]

You got it again, didn't you? There were other options, but in our moment they would have been even less effective:

- Piracy isn't fair to the creators of that content.
- Piracy is disloyal to your fellow citizens.
- Piracy is forbidden by the government.
- Piracy is a disgusting and evil act.

Instead of those, our culture argued that piracy *harms*. The moral reasoning of those seeking to get all of us to refrain from this act was to convince us that there is a victim being harmed out there in the world. We may not know who that victim is. But watch out—they're out there. And your downloading of music or movies is harming them.

This goes to show how we have been trained to think about right and wrong, and what we subconsciously prioritize.

CHANNELING JOHN STUART MILL

What we don't often realize when we say "Do whatever you want, as long as it doesn't hurt someone" is that we are kind of/almost quoting a famous philosopher named John Stuart Mill. He was influential in the political philosophy of liberalism, which argues citizens should

---

9 *hurt (i.e. "harm")*
10 *victimless*

be liberated from every restraint possible (and is the basis for our democracy). It consists of classical liberals (Republicans) and progressive liberals (Democrats).

His famous quote that we repeat without knowing it comes from his book *On Liberty*, written in 1859.

"The only purpose for which power can be rightfully exercised over any member of a civilised community, against his will, is to prevent harm to others."

John Stuart Mill

In Western culture, where we are the products of Enlightenment thinkers and philosophers like John Stuart Mill, we have a very finely tuned receptor to issues of care/harm. It's the primary way we tend to think about right and wrong. It's what we lean toward when we want to convince someone that they are wrong, because it tends to be the most effective strategy.

Care/harm is a massively important foundation for morality, that we would of course find lots of Scriptural backing for. But it's not the *only* category we find for morality throughout the Bible (as we will see from a single study on the Ten Commandments). And if it becomes our only functional category for determining right from wrong we are left in a bad spot.

We would end up confused by the first 4 commandments, who don't have an easily identifiable victim. We would end up confused about many things that the Scriptures prohibit, asking ourselves why God would forbid such a thing if it doesn't harm anyone? And at the end of that road, we may be tempted to believe that God Himself is the one doing the harming by not allowing people to do whatever they want as long as they aren't hurting anybody.

The simple reality is that a sole focus on issues of care/harm will leave a person, or a society, morally stunted.

MORAL DUMBFOUNDEDNESS & LOST LANGUAGES

One fascinating study Haidt conducted detailed in *The Righteous Mind* was meant to uncover something he calls "moral dumbfoundedness." He wanted to arrange experiments where people in our culture would intuitively believe something was wrong, but not have the language or categories to explain why it was wrong, leaving them morally dumbfounded.

With the goal to expose that our culture has lost clarity for certain categories of morality, Haidt intentionally tried to craft scenarios that would remove all conceivable harm and take away any possibility of a victim, yet still trigger people to condemn them. Here's one experiment he conducted:

> Julie and Mark, who are sister and brother, are traveling together in France. They are both on summer vacation from college. One night they are staying alone in a cabin near the beach. They decide that it would be interesting and fun if they tried making love. At the very least it would be a new experience for each of them. Julie is already taking birth control pills, but Mark uses a condom too, just to be safe. They both enjoy it, but they decide not to do it again. They keep that night as a special secret between them, which makes them feel even closer to each other. So what do you think about this? Was it wrong for them to have sex?[11]

How would you answer? If you were a non-Christian secular American, how would you go about reasoning through this?

20% of the subjects said it was fine for them to have sex, because they are both consenting adults, and no one was harmed. He talked about how other subjects would condemn it as wrong, but couldn't explain why so they flailed about looking for a victim to blame it on to be able to prove it was wrong. Here is a transcript of one subject's response:

- **Experimenter:** So what do you think about this, was it wrong for Julie and Mark to have sex?

- **Subject:** Yeah, I think it's totally wrong to have sex. You know, because I'm pretty religious and I just think incest is wrong anyway. But, I don't know.

- **Experimenter:** What's wrong with incest, would you say?

- **Subject:** Um, the whole idea of, well, I've heard—I don't even know if this is true, but in the case, if the girl did get pregnant, the kids become deformed, most of the time, in cases like that.

---

11 Jonathan Haidt, *The Righteous Mind*, p.45.

- **Experimenter:** But they used a condom and birth control pills—

- **Subject:** Oh, OK. Yeah, you did say that.

- **Experimenter:** —so there's no way they're going to have a kid.

- **Subject:** Well, I guess the safest sex is abstinence, but, um, uh...um, I don't know, I just think that's wrong. I don't know, what did you ask me?

- **Experimenter:** Was it wrong for them to have sex?

- **Subject:** Yeah, I think it's wrong.

- **Experimenter:** And I'm trying to find out why, what you think is wrong with it.

- **Subject:** OK, um...well...let's see, let me think about this. Um—how old were they?

- **Experimenter:** They were college age, around 20 or so.

- **Subject:** Oh, oh (looks disappointed). I don't know, I just...it's just not something you're brought up to do. It's just not—well, I mean I wasn't. I assume most people aren't (laughs). I just think that you shouldn't—I don't—I guess my reason is, um...just that, um...you're not brought up to do it. You don't see it. I don't think it's accepted. That's pretty much it.

- **Experimenter:** You wouldn't say anything you're not brought up to see is wrong, would you? For example, if you're not brought up to see women working outside the home, would you say that makes it wrong for women to work?

- **Subject:** Um...well...oh, gosh. This is hard. I really—um, I mean there's just no way I could change my mind but I just don't know how to—how to show what I'm feeling, what I feel about it. It's crazy![12]

Moral. Dumfoundedness. What an amazing picture of it.

Somewhere in this subject's mind he or she knew it was wrong, but they couldn't justify it because they couldn't find a victim who was harmed. The person is literally searching for a lost language that they can't seem to find. There is no category for something being wrong because it violates something sacred, is disrespectful to the God who created us, and degrading to the humans doing it.

---

12 Ibid, p.46–47

In a similar experiment designed to produce the same effect, the author crafted a different scenario. Say a man goes out and buys a live chicken. He first kills the chicken, and he plans to cook it and eat it the rest of the week. But before he butchers and cooks the dead chicken, he decides that he wants to have sex with it. Is that wrong?

He polled different groups to show differences in subcultures. When he surveyed his University of Pennsylvania students, 73% of them said it was morally permissible. One anonymous student stated this position clearly:

- "It's his chicken, he's eating it, nobody is getting hurt."

- Another said, "It's perverted, but if it's done in private, it's his right."

To show different subcultures, he also polled working class adults employed at his local McDonalds. He said that there, many of the respondents simply stared disbelievingly at him, like *"You mean you don't know why it's wrong to do that to a chicken? I have to explain this to you?"*[13]

A quote from the book illustrates this seesaw effect:

"In the past fifty years people in many Western societies have come to feel compassion in response to many more kinds of animal suffering, and they've come to feel disgust in response to many fewer kinds of sexual activity."[14]

So we care about a chicken's quality of life while they produce our eggs, but evidently once they are dead and can't feel pain, all bets are off.

No harm no...fowl?

There are obviously subsets and differences among various groups in the way they think, and can we just say, thank God for the McDonalds workers? But all of this goes to show something very insightful about the culture we inhabit. In a secular, post-Christian culture there is an incredibly heightened priority on the first foundation, the care/harm foundation, such that it has become a primary lens through which we think about right and wrong.

---

13 Ibid, p.111
14 Ibid, p.145

Sidenote: Adding to the confusion is the fact that our cultural view of "harm" is increasingly subjective, leaving less and less room for the inherent difficulty of human constraints. Something as simple as hurt feelings or restricted personal freedoms can now be popularly thought of as "harm" that is to be rejected with no further scrutiny. We are in danger of confusing hurt or hardship with harm.

And on the other side, the sanctity/degradation foundation, the bar hardly even registers anymore. It's like a lost language. The category of some things or acts being holy and sanctified and other things being degraded or evil is completely lost on us. This is a major reason why our culture profoundly struggles with the idea that we are sinners who deserve God's wrath.

WE'RE GONNA NEED MORE CATEGORIES TO UNDERSTAND GOD

The extreme elevation of care/harm and fairness as the primary category in thinking about right and wrong, with the correlating descent of sanctity/degradation on the other side is only one broad cultural comment to be made when thinking of these categories. Many more applications will be drawn throughout this book. But to start, the aforementioned studies and claims make the argument that we as a broad culture are in great danger of being significantly off balance in our thinking on morality.

If we do not have the moral resources and categories we need to condemn incest or bestiality, we are in trouble.

Case in point, Jonathan Haidt went on the popular podcast of Dax Shephard, Armchair Expert, to discuss his research.[15] The experiment about the brother and sister committing incest was discussed, and Dax stated that while he didn't think he could say they were wrong for what they did because it did not harm anyone, he wouldn't want to hang out with that brother and sister. Later on in the episode, his cohost condemned him for intolerance because he said he would not

---

15 Armchair Expert with Dax Shepard: EXPERTS ON EXPERT: Jonathan Haidt https://podcasts. apple.com/us/podcast/experts-on-expert-jonathan-haidt/id1345682353?i=1000425262012

want to go to the movies with that brother and sister. They went on to discuss how one would go about declaring that a person who developed a romantic relationship with a dolphin was wrong for doing so (no answer was given), and even brought up how one could condemn an act as unthinkable and grotesque as necrophilia.[16]

Dax and his co-host had language to describe some of these acts as "unhealthy," but no way to pronounce moral judgement on them without an obvious victim who was experiencing suffering. This attests to a sad irony that while the purveyors of a fully post-Christian culture think the dictates of Scripture are backwards and oppressive, the reality is they are the ones with a grotesque and stunted moral vision that lacks not only the moral fortitude but even the categories necessary to condemn despicable and degrading acts.

As God pursues modern people in post-Christian cultures, He literally has to rebirth lost languages and revive entire categories that have been culturally lost. The good news is, rebirth is exactly what God has always done as He brings sin-marred, spiritually dead children back to Himself.

THE DEPTH OF THE RICHES IN THE WISDOM AND KNOWLEDGE OF GOD

The God we see in Scripture is a towering Creator over all space, time, and history. After Paul proclaims that God has written His laws on the human heart in chapter 2 of Romans, Paul breaks out in praise in chapter 11 and declares "Oh, the depth of the riches and wisdom and knowledge of God! How unsearchable are his judgments and how inscrutable his ways!" (Romans 11:33).

Every human culture has their own bent on thinking about right and wrong, due to individuals at a certain place and time using their culturally-affected and sin-marred consciences to come up with their own codes and mantras. There are echoes of truth in many of them, because we are made in God's image and that image is not totally effaced by our sin. But there are also errors in all of them, and God's wisdom confronts them all in different ways.

This is something we generally want God to do...as long as it is correcting the wrongs in *other* cultures we so easily see. But if we want those divine fingers

---

16 Necrophilia is sexual attraction and activity with a corpse.

pointed outward at the harmful things we see in other societies, they have to be able to point at our moral framework as well. If we have the freedom to dismiss the points we don't like, then everyone has the freedom to dismiss the points they don't like, and we're back to Genesis 3—thinking we've stripped God and the Bible of the authority to confront anything anywhere.

We are modern, enlightened, people living in an historically advanced culture and often can begin to think that we are the apex of civilization. But the fact is, we have enormous cultural blind spots and there are ways God's manifold wisdom forcefully confronts our thinking.

In order to see God and ourselves rightly, we are going to have to do something that isn't common: humble ourselves. And then see that God has a vision for the flourishing of humanity that is far more beautiful and multifaceted than a secular American would ever come up with. No level of adherence to vague "non-commandments" would ever accomplish God's dream for the world.

God's vision for people honoring Him and each other and existing in perfect harmony requires more than the pithy mandate of the harm principle: do whatever you want as long as it doesn't harm anyone.

Of course God cares about care/harm principles. His anger is often directed at violations of this through Scripture. But He also has robust categories for fairness, loyalty, authority, and sanctity. He alone is wise enough to hold all of those concerns in the perfect proportions and tease out how they interact. Or more accurately, these categories can only come to their true and proper interactions when they operate as God created them to.

And in the Ten Commandments, we see a beautiful re-assertion of the loving wisdom of God that our first parents threw off and sought to redefine in the Garden of Eden.

Consider how we can see evidence of these hard-wired moral categories highlighted through the Ten Commandments.[17] (These connections will be highlighted in the chapter on each commandment that follows.)

---

17 One could argue different combinations of these foundations throughout the Ten Commandments, but we've simply chosen the one or two that seems most obvious.

MORAL FOUNDATIONS HIGHLIGHTED IN THE TEN COMMANDMENTS

1. You shall have no other gods before me. ——————————

AUTHORITY LOYALTY

2. You shall not make for yourself a carved image, or any likeness of anything that is in heaven above, or that is in the earth beneath, or that is in the water under the earth. You shall not bow down to them or serve them, for I the Lord your God am a jealous God, visiting the iniquity of the fathers on the children to the third and the fourth generation of those who hate me, but showing steadfast love to thousands of those who love me and keep my commandments.

SANCTITY LOYALTY

3. You shall not take the name of the Lord your God in vain, for the Lord will not hold him guiltless who takes his name in vain.

SANCTITY

4. Remember the Sabbath day, to keep it holy. Six days you shall labor, and do all your work, but the seventh day is a Sabbath to the Lord your God. On it you shall not do any work...

SANCTITY

5. Honor your father and your mother, that your days may be long in the land that the Lord your God is giving you.

AUTHORITY

6. You shall not murder. ——————————————

CARE/HARM SANCTITY

7. You shall not commit adultery. ——————————

LOYALTY CARE/HARM

8. You shall not steal. ——————————————

FAIRNESS

9. You shall not bear false witness against your neighbor.

FAIRNESS CARE/HARM

10. You shall not covet your neighbor's house; you shall not covet your neighbor's wife, or his male servant, or his female servant, or his ox, or his donkey, or anything that is your neighbor's.

SANCTITY LOYALTY

These commandments consist of a list of just 10 items, yet draw from various categories for right and wrong. Most are negative—things not to do—while two of them are positive (keep the Sabbath holy and honor your father and mother). Most are actions, one is a desire (do not covet). Some have identifiable victims, others don't (other than God, whom our sin is primarily an offense against). The most famous list of laws in history draws from some foundations that feel utterly natural to us, and also others that are more like a lost language.

And remember, if given the opportunity to live in a community where everyone always kept all ten—most of us would jump at the chance.

REDUCED CATEGORIES & BIBLE CONFUSION

A robust understanding of God's multi-faceted wisdom and aim for human flourishing, paired with sufficient insight into your own culture, suddenly makes a lot of things that once may have been confusing fall into place.

There are many things in Scripture that, when approached by a modern American, are hard to make sense of. Certain commands or stories are often pulled out to be used as "gotcha passages" by non-believing people to say some version of, "See! Your God and His rules are ridiculous."

The dietary and clothing restrictions found throughout the ceremonial laws of Leviticus can be confusing to us, even though New Testament believers are no longer under the ceremonial laws of Judaism. But still... why would it matter if people wore clothing made with two different kinds of fabric (Leviticus 19:19)? Or what type of sea creatures were okay to eat (Leviticus 9:10)? However, when you consider that God was seeking to create a holy people who were sanctified or "set apart" for Himself, those things have a logical category to fit in. Israel was to be different from all other nations surrounding them who did not worship God and submit to His authority.

The same is true for the elaborate cleansing rituals the priests and the people of God were instructed to go through to worship God. We read those accounts and they almost feel bizarre, like a case-study in OCD. But the reality is God is so holy and pure that those incredibly involved rituals make all the sense in the world if not for Jesus. If we rightly perceived how majestically pure God is, we would recognize these rituals as 'fitting' or 'reasonable.' We might even balk at the flippant approaches to God our culture tends to produce.[18]

When Hebrews tells us that we can have direct access to the throne of grace because Jesus has become the new high priest, offering the sacrifice of Himself once and for all—that is supposed to be the shocking, jaw-dropping reality.[19] We should not be shocked by the fact that God's people had to follow incredibly detailed instructions to approach His holiness.

One common argument points out that God's responses sometimes feel disproportionate or too harsh. A popular example is the flood of the Earth described in Genesis 6. "What could have possibly prompted such a response?" modern minds (who care primarily about care/harm of individuals) think. Those thinkers grab the judge's gavel and pronounce that no collective act could have justified such a response by God.

And they do so with an extremely culturally-affected, one-sided framework for morality that just so happens to have a very diminished concern for matters of sanctity and authority. So they read right past the verses that explain:

> The Lord saw that the wickedness of man was great in the earth, and that every intention of the thoughts of his heart was only evil continually. 6 And the Lord regretted that he had made man on the earth, and it grieved him to his heart.[20]

Every intention of the thoughts of his heart was only evil...continually.

The evil of those people had been so great and unrestrained that their continued presence was degrading the Earth and inhibiting God's design for creation. And God as creator was perfectly just in His response. A proper understanding of God's authority and concern for the sanctity of his creation explains why He chose to restart His creation with the family of Noah that had found favor in His eyes.

A similar argument is often made about God commanding the Israelites to wipe out surrounding people groups in war. That is declared an unconscionable act that merits judgment upon God. But the question is not often asked: *What kinds of people populated those nations? Why did God command such a thing? And what effect would they have had on Israel if that were not commanded?*

---

18 See: Jesus is my homeboy shirts.
19 Hebrews chapters 4 & 7
20 Genesis 6:5-6

We fancy those nations as simple, good-hearted primitive people that were just trying to survive. But just to give one example, the nation of Ammon worshipped the god of Molech and practiced child-sacrifice as we discussed earlier. God warned the Israelites that anyone who sacrificed their children to Molech would be put to death[21], but even still the practice crept in, culminating with Solomon, who built a statue of Molech in a high place so his foreign wives could worship their false god.[22]

Sometimes things that are very difficult for us to understand are made more clear by zooming far out of our cultural lenses and seeing that God has more categories for morality than we often have.[23] He is seeking to re-establish His rightful authority and working toward the flourishing of a people united to Him, not simply to free humans to do as they please. That is not an effort worth God's time and energy.

Because of that aim, certain things are a way bigger deal to Him than they seem to us, and that's because we are wrong and narrow-minded, not Him. His response is not irrational or extreme, but right and holy.

Many Americans tend to think God's wrath isn't *fair*, showing our heightened moral category for that concern. But part of that reasoning is because we don't think sin is that big of a deal—and certainly not sins that don't seem to harm someone. We don't care as much that people violently rebel against God's authority, betray His loyalty, or degrade and debase the holy—so we don't think of those things as deserving of wrath. In God's vision all of those things are serious offenses, and sometimes deserving of swift wrath, death, and even eternal separation from Him. All of which makes the sacrifice of Jesus that enables us to approach God's throne with confidence all the more astounding.

On the other side of that, potentially things that seem like a very big deal to us are sometimes less so to Him, because He has more categories than we do. For example: in our culture, sexual restraint due to a pursuit of holiness and sanctity feels like unbearable and unreasonable suffering. (And if it harms someone, it must be wrong.)

---

21 Leviticus 20:2, 4-5

22 1 Kings 11:6-8

23 There are, to be clear, difficult, or obscure things to deal with in the Bible and this resource or explanation of moral categories will not seek to deal with all of them. For further research, the book *Is God a Moral Monster?* by Paul Copan is a helpful resource.

Scripture does not give us that idea, however. We find empathy, communal support, eternal perspective, and supernatural help through the Holy Spirit for the difficult crosses we are called to bear—but not evidence that if God calls someone to sexual restraint that He is wrong and oppressive.

In short, many of the things we find so hard to understand about God are explained when we see that God is much bigger, has more moral categories, and has a much more beautiful vision for human flourishing than America does.

He intends to re-create the paradise we forsook in Genesis 3 and train sons and daughters to enjoy His Kingdom forever. The only way to be a part of that re-creation is to place ourselves fully under His authority and trust that He is wiser than our culturally-formed perceptions. He has not asked us to trust that blindly, but has put forth the blood of His own Son Jesus to prove that He is for our good.

INTERLUDE 2
SECULARISM: LEARNING TO SEE OURSELVES

"There are these two young fish swimming along and they happen to meet an older fish swimming the other way, who nods at them and says "Morning, boys. How's the water?" And the two young fish swim on for a bit, and then eventually one of them looks over at the other and goes "What the h*** is water?"

David Foster Wallace

We are one culture among many who currently inhabit the Earth, among many more who have existed through history. Each one has had trouble seeing themselves clearly.

Through travel, education, cross-cultural relationships, movies, and art one can learn to "see" other cultures, to start to trace out how they are different from yours, and that can start to give shape to how you see your own. But even still, for a fish—it's very difficult to understand what water is.

The water of a particular culture is its worldview.

> **Worldview** - The set of ideas that an individual or culture views the world and reality through, that is often invisible to them (like a fish in water).

So we have a worldview, and it's particular to our time and place. It's markedly different from the people in the Bible, and different from people across the globe.

For example, many cultures around the world today think much more collectively than we do, where groups like families, teams, companies, tribes, and nations are more than the sum of the individuals that compose them. In these cultures institutions matter, must be protected, and people have an obligation to play their assigned roles for the good of the group. Collectivist cultures have a much, much higher value for group loyalty than we do. If you grew up in a culture like this, odds are you wouldn't ever do anything that put yourself ahead of the group. Doing so would be seen as selfish and foolish, dangerously risking the health and safety of the group you care about more than yourself.

One member of our church who has an Asian American cultural background said that in their culture, it was viewed as wrong for you not to live near your parents, because when you grow up it's now your role to take care of your parents.

So stop and think: would secular American culture say that it is wrong to do something that puts yourself ahead of the group you happen to belong to? That doing so would be selfish and foolish of you?

Ummm...no.

We are the exact opposite! We actually teach people that loyalty is dangerous. That individuals *must* put themselves ahead of the group. Because the most important thing in all of life is for you to become the most true version of you, and you can't let anyone or anything get in the way of that. This is basically every single Disney movie, from Moana throwing off the constraints of a small island life to Kung Fu Panda leaving behind the family noodle shop to go be a ninja.

You may hear a voice inside
And if the voice starts to whisper
To follow the farthest star
Moana, that voice inside is
Who you are.

Moana

So that starts to give you a clue about what we prioritize, and how we are set apart from other cultures that prioritize other concerns.

Professor Richard Sweder and his research partners give a simple breakdown of how worldviews have different starting points and therefore different outworkings of morality.[24] They give 3 basic categories: a starting ethic of autonomy, community, and divinity.

---

24 "The 'Big Three' of Morality (Autonomy, Community, Divinity) and the 'Big Three' Explanations of Suffering" https://psycnet.apa.org/record/1997-05770-006

	Autonomy	Community	Divinity
The human body is...	A playground	A machine part	A temple[25]
The greatest sin is...	Abuse/ Intolerance	Disloyalty/ Betrayal	Degrading or Profane Acts
The conception of the self is similar to...	An avocado	A grape	A seed
Moral categories that will be prioritized...	Care/Harm & Fairness	Loyalty & Authority	Sanctity & Authority

An ethic of autonomy starts with and prioritizes the individual. Some conclusions that could be drawn here are that the human body in this worldview is like a playground—primarily something to be enjoyed. As Anthony Bourdain said, "Your body is not a temple, it's an amusement park. Enjoy the ride."

The greatest sins here are abuse or mistreatment of individuals, or the intolerance of not allowing them the freedom to express themselves. The conception of the human self here is like that of an avocado: a somewhat frail outer layer, with a really solid inner core that one must be true to at all costs.[26] This type of culture will emphasize issues of harm and fairness in morality.

An ethic of community starts with a group bigger than oneself, and the self is subject to the good of the group and the interconnectedness of the others involved. Self-sacrifice for the group will be necessary and celebrated. The greatest sin here is disloyalty to the bigger group, and the conception of the self is like a grape: interconnected to the other grapes on the stem, and it's not of great importance to be unique or differentiated from the other grapes. This type of culture will prioritize issues of loyalty and authority in morality.

---

25 These 3 metaphors come from *The Righteous Mind*, p.175.
26 The idea of the Western self being like an avocado and the Eastern self being like a grape came from this video. Philosophies of Self: East-West Distinctions | Gish Jen https://www.youtube.com/watch?v=mabjJJDqjFM The metaphor of a seed was added.

An ethic of divinity starts with the divine and sees humans as bearers of a god-like image that must be guarded. The human body is a temple in this worldview, so there are ways one should act and not act in order to reflect the holiness of the divine life-giver. The conception of the self is more like that of a seed—something that must be sewn in self-sacrifice in order to be raised to what it was created to be by the divine. This type of society will lean toward sanctity and authority in moral thinking.

It's not necessary to even ask what our culture is. We are the most autonomous of autonomous cultures that have ever autonomously lived on this green and blue sphere.

We prioritize the rights of the individual to limitless degrees, seeking to throw off any and every structure that might keep free individuals from being whomever they want to be and doing whatever they want to do. We live in a place and time that trains us from the stories we hear early on that the most important thing is to follow your heart, no matter what it says. And those messages have sunk down so deep to our very cores that they can pass for reality and not be seen for what they are: *ideas*. A particular worldview in a particular time and place, rather unique among human history.

So, 2 questions emerge:

1. **How do we name and describe the cultural water we are swimming in?** What are some helpful descriptors and language that we can use to start to see our culture more clearly?

2. **How did we get here?** What particular historical factors led us to arrive at this place?

Question #1: How do we name and describe the cultural water we are swimming in?

Answer: Secularism

Secularism has various meanings, and used in the political sphere simply refers to the separation of church and state.

But the catch-all term has been used widely by theologians to describe post-Christian cultures that, on the whole, are moving away from baseline belief in the supernatural and wide acceptance of divine authority. In many ways it is synonymous with post-Christianity.

Charles Taylor, the foremost Christian scholar on secularism, defines it as "a move from a society where belief in God is unchallenged and indeed, unproblematic, to one in which it is understood to be one option among others, and frequently not the easiest to embrace."

In a secular culture, belief in God is not necessarily denied or prohibited, but placed on a buffet line of reasonable choices one can use to make sense of life and give meaning and purpose. But it really doesn't matter so long as that belief is privatized, and the big issue isn't that people don't believe in God, but that they simply don't care.

Here is the way we would succinctly describe it:

> **Secularism** - A post-Enlightenment way of viewing God and the spiritual realm. It's baseline posture is skepticism and apathy toward the supernatural, with little respect for God's authority.

If that feels a little fuzzy, the next question will hopefully put some skin around the idea.

Question #2: How did we get here?

Answer: Western Secular Liberalism

In short, we arrived here through a time period called the Enlightenment that had profound effects on Western Civilization and the founding ideas of America. If you haven't seen it yet, or even if you have, go to ForOurGoodAlways.com and watch the video called Western Secular Liberalism. This video attempts to describe the historical forces and events that created the water we swim in.

Here's a quick summary of the video's conclusions:

Western - A way of viewing the world that highlights the centrality of the individual and the rights for those individuals to be self-defining and autonomous. (As opposed to more Eastern or pre-Western worldviews that were centered around a collective community or the divine.)

Secular - A post-Enlightenment way of viewing God and the spiritual realm. It's baseline posture is doubt and skepticism of anything supernatural and a rejection of God's authority.

Liberalism - The political ideology that prioritizes the freedom (liberty) of the individuals that make up a society and forms the basis for democracy. The driving force is that people are by nature good, and should be free from any arbitrary restraint, tyranny, or oppressor. (It encompasses what we call Republicans, who tend to prioritize the freedom of their finances, businesses, the market, and our nation—as well as Democrats, who tend to prioritize the freedom of restraints on an individual's body, sexual expression, or other restraints like gender.)

It may be helpful to think of liberalism as "freedomism." This showcases that the driving force is ultimately about freedom of the individual, and that it's not just found on the political left.

(But really—go watch the video if you haven't. The summaries aren't enough without the historical context.)

Important note: Through the remainder of the book, we will be using "secularism" as a catch-all term for our cultural direction, for simplicity and consistency with outside voices. And because Western Secular Liberalism is a mouthful to say.

But when you read the term throughout the book, think of the video and all the implications our worldview has about belief in God, human authority/government, and human nature.

If you are more of the reading type, you can find the transcript of the video in Appendix 1.

THE ENLIGHTENMENT
WHY WE THINK THE WAY WE DO

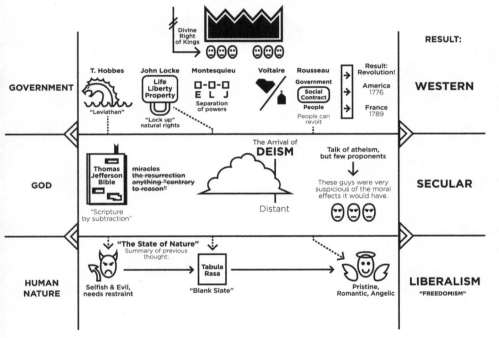

CHAPTER 3
WHY YOU MAY NOT BE A CHRISTIAN IN 10 YEARS

"There is a common, worldly kind of Christianity in this day, which many have, and think they have enough—a cheap Christianity which offends nobody, and requires no sacrifice—which costs nothing, and is worth nothing."

J.C. Ryle

THERE'S SOMETHING IN THE WATER

There are strong currents in the water we swim in, and they are not going toward God. There are powerful forces at play under the surface, swirling around, that are incompatible with biblical Christianity.

To be clear: no culture has ever been perfectly set up to receive the wisdom and authority of God. People who pine for the "good ole days" in America forget that the 1950s had massive issues of their own, detestable racial injustice being a primary one. So don't hear this chapter as a longing for way back when everything was perfect, because it never was.

There are many things to celebrate in our culture, and many things that God would affirm. He deeply cares about injustice, oppression, and harms done to His image bearers, as long as He gets to define how we apply those terms.

But this book is not focused on the strengths of our culture, or even the ways we may need further application of those in our culture. It is, rather, focused on the blind spots, the weaknesses, the things we may not see or notice—of which there are many.

The most dangerous currents, after all, are the ones you can't see.

DE-CONVERSION STORIES

Since the New Testament, conversion stories have been a powerful means of spreading the gospel. When people proclaim their journey—how they used to live and operate outside of God, what God did to get their attention, and how He saved them through the work of Jesus—it can be a tremendously helpful way to understand the truth of the gospel.

However, in recent decades and years, the polar opposite has become popular as well. In an article for The Gospel Coalition, Michael J. Kruger expounds on this topic:

> De-conversion stories are designed not to reach non-Christians but to reach Christians. And their purpose is to convince them that their outdated, naïve beliefs are no longer worthy of their assent. A person simply shares his testimony of how he once thought like you did but has now seen the light.
>
> Of course, there have always been de-conversion stories throughout church history—if one would only take the time to dig them up and listen to them. Christianity has never had a shortage of people who were once in the fold and then left.
>
> In recent years, however, these de-conversion stories seem to have taken on a higher profile. Part of this is due, no doubt, to the technology that makes them more available, whether through podcasts, blogs, or other forms of media.
>
> But it's also due to the fact that many of those who de-convert have realized a newfound calling to share their testimony with as many people as possible. Rather than just quietly leaving their old beliefs and moving on to new ones—something that would have been more common in prior generations—a new guard seems to have made it their life's ambition to evangelize the found.
>
> Indeed, many of these de-conversion stories are told with the kind of conviction, passion, and evangelistic zeal that would make a modern televangelist blush. In their minds, they're missionaries to the "lost" in every sense of the word. They just have to help these Christians realize they are mistaken and lead them to the truth.[27]

---

27 "Jen Hatmaker and the Power of De-Conversion Stories" https://www.thegospelcoalition.org/article/jen-hatmaker-power-deconversion-stories/

These de-conversion stories vary in landing place. Some go all the way to atheism or agnosticism. Others still identify with the label "Christian" but abandon essential tenets of Christianity. Others, like the primary subject of Kruger's article Jen Hatmaker, abandon the sexual ethic of Scripture for progressive ethics accepted by modern culture.

And that acceptance by culture is a telling component of these stories. Jesus said that His followers would not be accepted by the world, but the de-converted certainly seem to be (John 15:18-25). When these deflections happen, non-believers and secular media outlets surround with admiration and applause, lifting up those voices to new platforms.

Kruger outlines an instructive 5 step playbook apparent in most of these de-conversion stories:

1. Recount the negatives of your fundamentalist past.
2. Position yourself as the offended party who bravely fought the establishment.
3. Portray your opponents as overly dogmatic while you are just a seeker.
4. Insist your new theology is driven by the Bible and is not a rejection of it.
5. Attack the character of your old group and uplift the character of your new group.

Utilizing Haidt's moral categories, you can trace a clear pattern among these stories. There is a clear rejection of God's authority found in Scripture, with a corresponding break from the tradition of the Christian church through the past two millennia. There is sharp disagreement with what God says is acceptable in human behavior, negating the God-defined parameters for sanctity. And all of this is done in the name of human rights, with a desire to prevent perceived "harm" from undue restrictions.

It's not surprising, because it perfectly reflects our culture.

This group of de-converted ones, is wide-ranging and uses different labels. The most dangerous ones are those that still use the term Christian or "progressive Christian," but do not match up with Scripture's portrayal of one who is reconciled to God through faith in Jesus and therefore happily accepts God's authority over their life.

Examples range from:

- Rob Bell, who was a popular Christian pastor and author a decade ago, but who has rejected biblical Christianity for a vague spiritualism that even Oprah can applaud.

- The late Rachel Held Evans, popular blogger and author, who still claimed the title Christian, but also proclaimed "Paul was wrong about some s***."[28]

- The hosts of the popular podcast The Liturgists, aimed at the spiritually disenfranchised. This includes Michael Gungor, formerly of the band Gungor, who now goes by a Hindu name, and Hilary McBride who uses Christian terminology but recently stated "The reason Jesus came is to save us from the idea that we are bad."[29]

- Nadia Bolz Weber, a self-described "public theologian" who started a church in Denver. She claimed on a podcast with Pete Holmes, former youth pastor and star of the HBO show *Crashing*, that in 10 years of pastoring her church she never once "told people what to do with their junk."[30] She believes the idea of God having wrath is punitive and unthinkable, doesn't believe that Jesus necessarily physically existed or raised from the dead, but that "death and resurrection is a powerful metaphor" and "the gospel is still the truest story I've ever heard." She also claims that watching porn is fine as long as it is "ethically-sourced porn," and while leading her church had a position for a drag queen Minister of Fabulousness.[31]

- Though less of a public figure in theological circles, comedian Pete Holmes also detailed his de-conversion in the podcast mentioned above and stated that the first threesome he ever had was "the most spiritual experience I've ever had."

- Joshua Harris, who also used to be a popular pastor and author of dating and marriage books, who announced his de-conversion (and

---

28 The Liturgists podcast: Christian (Part 1) https://theliturgists.com/podcast/2018/9/20/christian-part-1
29 The Liturgists podcast: Does Being Good Mean My Beliefs Shouldn't Change? https://theliturgists.com/podcast/2020/2/6/does-being-good-mean-my-beliefs-shouldnt-change
30 You Made It Weird with Pete Holmes: Nadia Bolz-Weber https://podcasts.apple.com/us/podcast/nadia-bolz-weber/id475878118?i=1000435125010
31 Liberal Lutheran pastor: It's okay to look at porn, especially if it's 'ethically sourced' https://www.lifesitenews.com/news/lutheran-pastor-its-okay-to-look-at-porn-especially-if-its-ethically-source

separation from his wife) on Instagram and apologized for the damage his writing and ministry caused to people.[32] (Note the care/harm foundation he used to apologize.) He, thankfully, had the integrity to clearly say he cannot consider himself a Christian:

"I have undergone a massive shift in regard to my faith in Jesus. The popular phrase for this is "deconstruction," the biblical phrase is "falling away." By all the measurements that I have for defining a Christian, I am not a Christian. Many people tell me that there is a different way to practice faith and I want to remain open to this, but I'm not there now."

Joshua Harris

It is an unfortunate blessing when someone de-converting is honest enough to say this, because it reduces the confusion rampant when someone can apparently believe anything and still publicly be considered "Christian." What is sad, however, in Joshua Harris' announcement is that he actually realized what he was doing, ending his post with a quote from Martin Luther about repentance and clearly stating that is what he understood himself to be doing—just that the repentance was *away* from Christianity—not *to* it.

These de-conversions eerily follow the outworkings of the "ethic of Autonomy" discussed earlier. The human individual is sovereign and sacrosanct (too holy to be interfered with). It exists for pleasure and happiness and any restrictions perceived to restrict that pursuit are oppressive and must be thrown off, no matter where they come from. The cardinal sin is telling someone that they are wrong, because WHO ARE YOU to do that to a sovereign self that must be true to itself at any cost? Issues of perceived harm will be prioritized over any other concern—even if said "harm" proceeds from dictates of God that have the goal of eternal good.

	Autonomy
The human body is...	A playground
The greatest sin is...	Abuse/Intolerance
The conception of the self is similar to...	An avocado
Moral categories that will be prioritized...	Care/Harm & Fairness/Cheating

32 Joshua Harris on Instagram https://www.instagram.com/p/B0ZBrNLH2sl/?utm_source=ig_embed

In this framework, when you disagree with God, you win. He is not allowed to confront you. You either creatively change what He says to agree with you, or if you can't do that—you dethrone Him.

In case you think this is largely a reaction against distant cultural figures in Christianity, we would be sad to inform you that this all has hit our church very close to home. Our pastors could tell you story after story of beloved members who once seemed to vibrantly trust and walk with Jesus, who now have rejected Him exactly along many of these lines. It is a heartbreaking trend nationwide and in our backyard, and seems to represent one of the greatest spiritual threats aimed at the flocks we are called to shepherd and protect. The effects of secularism are so powerful and dangerous because they are very difficult to see for what they are.

DECONSTRUCTION AS A CONTINUATION

In the academic field, deconstruction is a form of textual criticism aimed at tearing down the meaning of a text or language, originating from French philosopher Jacques Derrida. Depending on the interpretation it can border on the absurd, questioning the possibility of any text having a clear and true meaning. Richard Ellman defines deconstruction as "the systematic undoing of understanding."[33]

On a popular level, it is simply used as a descriptor for the process described above. By those claiming to go through deconstruction, it is generally painted in a positive light, as if unhelpful things are being torn down. And to be sure, depending on one's background and belief systems, a process of "tearing down" could be quite necessary and helpful. Lies about God and the world always need to be torn down and replaced with the truth.

But in this realm, deconstruction is often the authority of God being torn down. And that's not overstatement—the term "deconstruct" literally means to take apart, tear down. Zooming out to think about our collective history, this is not surprising. It is a continuation of two things:

1. A continuation of Satan's oldest lie.

The oldest lie was that God cannot be trusted, that He is not in fact for our good. Deconstruction started with Satan as he sought to tear down God's

---

33 Deconstruction http://www.gutenberg.cc/articles/Deconstruction

beautiful world and the intimate friendship He intended to have with the image bearers He created. Consider the infamous words that proceeded from the serpent's mouth: "Did God actually say, 'You shall not eat of any tree in the garden?'" (Gen 3:1). The devil's strategy starts by questioning what God clearly said to introduce confusion or distrust.

This is not new. What is relatively new is that Satan has deceived us into not just declaring independence from God, but using morality to actually pronounce judgment upon Him. Pastor John Mark Comer from Portland remarked that when he was a teenager, his non-Christian friends didn't share his sexual ethic but thought the Christian sexual ethic was higher, or more holy than theirs—they just didn't want it. Now, he says, his non-Christian friends see the Christian sex ethic as lower than theirs—as backwards and repressive.

Satan has begun to use the harm principle against God, constantly accusing that His laws will hurt us, and not lead to our flourishing. He uses our swollen, one-sided morality categories to lob horrible untruths about God.

He accuses us before God...and he also accuses God before us.

Nadia Bolz-Weber's writing makes this extraordinarily clear and simple:

"If the teachings of the church are harming people, then we need to rethink those teachings."[34]

In her book, *Shameless: the Sexual Revolution* she calls out "harm that's been done to people as a result of what the church has taught them about sex, body, and gender." She explains: "You can draw a straight f***ing line from what people were told in church and the harm in their lives."[35]

The argument could not be made any clearer: if God's design for human flourishing conflicts with what humans think flourishing is, and therefore causes them perceived "harm," He must be done away with or redefined.

---

34 "Liberal Lutheran pastor: It's okay to look at porn, especially if it's 'ethically sourced'" https://www.lifesitenews.com/news/lutheran-pastor-its-okay-to-look-at-porn-especially-if-its-ethically-source

35 In the same article, she mentions instigating an art project where women mail her their purity rings so she can turn them into a sculpture of a vagina.

2. A continuation of Enlightenment values.

When you step back to look at it, this also becomes undeniable. We've been tearing down authority we don't like for centuries. We are revolutionaries at heart. We don't trust Kings, and that becomes a problem when God describes Himself as just that (Revelation 19:16).

We are freedom fighters by nature and nurture, living in a culture that has trained us from the beginning of its existence to fight to protect our rights at all costs. As Sam Elder-Bell remarked, often "Political emancipation is a stop on the road to human emancipation."

We want the Kingdom, and all the benefits and privileges that come with it. But we don't want the King.

The sad reality is that all this deconstruction does not in fact leave us with the Kingdom we want, but with our own paltry and sad kingdoms where we get to reign (and possibly newly formed and powerless churches that align with beliefs we've created). We trade the promise of bedrock joy in Christ now and forever for the fickle acceptance of culture and a few decades of measly freedom on our own terms. Those in the wake of deconstruction often wind up in a gospel-less story foretold in these words by Richard Neibuhr, where:

"A God without wrath brought men without sin into a kingdom without judgment through the ministrations of a Christ without a cross."[36]

WHAT ARE THEY CONVERTING TO?

It's not enough to call them de-conversion stories, and it's not sufficient to stop at deconstruction. The people, whom God dearly loves, that are going through this do not tear all they previously held down and then stand in the midst of nothingness.

No—their de-conversions are really a conversion. Their deconstruction tears down one worldview and substitutes another.

In Joshua Harris's announcement, this is quite apparent. He repents of being a Christian and the potentially "harmful" effects his teaching had on people, asks for forgiveness from certain people groups (in a similar

36 "What's Left of Liberalism?" https://theoutline.com/post/7687/what-is-left-of-liberalism-ah-mari-french?zd=1&zi=znj6yxzl

fashion as people repenting to Christianity ask forgiveness from God). And then he implicitly asks for inclusion in the group he is deflecting to. It's trading one religion for another.

So what do we call the religion these adherents are deflecting to?

One could argue different labels, but broadly speaking they are converting to the spirit of the age—secularism. Freedomism: a religion, a worldview, where there is nothing more sovereign than the individual and his or her rights, who is by nature good instead of sinful, and will only be happy if freed from all self-described constraints.

In short, the religion they are converting to looks exactly like the world around them. Which is why it sounds so hollow when these people are praised for their courage while they celebrate what everyone else affirms.

CALLED OUT OF THE WORLD TO REACH IT

Israel was called out of the world by God in the Old Testament to be His people, under His re-established authority on Earth, and showcase what human flourishing truly looks like as a nation of priests, or representatives of God (Exodus 19:6). This old covenant was instructive and important, but insufficient, because it was based on their ability to obey God's laws—which they were continually unable to do—and a sacrificial system that could never fully take away their sins. As the writer of Hebrews notes "it is impossible for the blood of bulls and goats to take away sin" (Hebrews 10:4).

The New Covenant instituted by Jesus fulfills all the intentional inadequacies of the Old Covenant, where Jesus becomes the great high priest mediating between God and man and the once-for-all sacrifice for sin (Hebrews 7:26-28). This covenant is sealed by grace alone, through faith in Christ (Ephesians 2:8).

The Greek word for church is *ekklesia*, and it means "called out ones." We are called out of the world and through repentance and faith enter the Kingdom of God, where we trust God to know what is best for ourselves and others.

Jesus, while praying to the Father for his disciples in John 17, says this:

> *I have given them your word, and the world has hated them*
> *because they are not of the world, just as I am not of the world.* ₁₅
> *I do not ask that you take them out of the world, but that you keep*
> *them from the evil one.* ₁₆ *They are not of the world, just as I am*
> *not of the world.* ₁₇ *Sanctify them in the truth; your word is truth.* ₁₈
> *As you sent me into the world, so I have sent them into the world.*

John 17:14-18

Jesus was also hated by the culture He inhabited, which led to Him being killed. He acknowledges that He had given His people God's truth, and that they would be hated and disliked by the cultures they find themselves in just as He was, because we would not look like the world or affirm its values.

He prays for God to sanctify us in the truth and be kept from the influence of the evil one, so that we would not be "of the world" just as He was not of the world. And also so that we would be sent into the world as a purified counter-culture, stable enough to be a powerful witness of God's grace and wisdom.

As His called-out ones, we are called to repent from what the Bible calls "worldliness," not succumb to it. (Which is exactly what the de-converted are doing.) We are called to pray for protection against the influence of the world on us, not to uncritically embrace the world until we reflect enough of its values for it to applaud us.

The unfortunate reality is that, increasingly so, the faith of many self-described Christians is not strong enough to withstand the powerful currents all around us. Our leaders, our neighbors, and our friends are being colonized by the world. Overtaken by it.

We do not want that for any of us, and the prayer of Jesus shows that He doesn't desire that either. He wants His *ekklesia* to be pure, with single-minded devotion to God's kingship and continual repentance when we stray. He wants us to be so soaked in God's truth that we are strong enough to be whimsical and stable missionaries to a culture that increasingly doesn't like or understand us, and not be in danger of succumbing to the tide.

He wants that for the good of all of those people out there in the world that He dearly loves, that He came to give His life for.

> *When he saw the crowds, he had compassion for them, because they were harassed and helpless, like sheep without a shepherd. ₃₇ Then he said to his disciples, "The harvest is plentiful, but the laborers are few; ₃₈ therefore pray earnestly to the Lord of the harvest to send out laborers into his harvest."*

Matthew 9:36-38

This is why we constantly and repeatedly call each other to repentance, why we proclaim God's word even when it is hard, why we arrange everything we do corporately to soak us in God's truth and expose lies. This is why we call our people to daily spiritual practices, so we can learn how to follow Jesus in ordinary life together, and not be colonized by our culture.

So that in 10 years we will not only still be Christians, but stronger, wiser and more vibrant Christians, full of grace and truth and hope for a world that will continue to need it more than ever.

INTERLUDE 3
THE UNIQUE MORALS OF SECULARISM

"We need the wisdom of the communion of saints. They broaden our perspective beyond our current culture and time. 'Every age has its own outlook,' C. S. Lewis wrote. 'It is specially good at seeing certain truths and specially liable to make certain mistakes.' By focusing on what's current, we rob ourselves of the insights and questions of those who have gone before us."

Peter Leithart, *The Ten Commandments*

If you were asked who you thought the weirdest people in the world were, what would come to your mind? Maybe a type of culture that you have particular trouble understanding, or possibly some cultish group with obscure practices you saw a documentary about?

What if someone were to argue that, objectively speaking about history, the answer is actually...

Us?

In 2010, cultural psychologists Joseph Henrich, Steven Heine, and Ara Norenzayan published a research paper titled "The Weirdest People in the World?"[37] In this paper, they discussed what they called WEIRD cultures, which stands for:

Western
Educated
Industrialized
Rich
Democratic

---

37 "The weirdest people in the world?" Behavioral and Brain Sciences https://www.cambridge.org/core/journals/behavioral-and-brain-sciences/article/weirdest-people-in-the-world/BF84F-7517D56AFF7B7EB58411A554C17

Sidenote: Remember, *Western* infers an ethic of autonomy and individualism spawned from the Enlightenment, and it stands in contrast to the cultures with a dominant ethic of community (such as Eastern cultures today) and those with a dominant ethic of divinity (such as some Middle Eastern cultures). WEIRD cultures add the dynamics of being highly educated, industrialized instead of pre-modern or agrarian, comparatively wealthy, and democratic—all of which profoundly shapes the ways in which people think.

The abstract for their paper gives a broad overview of their research, with a surprising claim. The authors argue that most of the psychological research in human history has been performed on subjects from WEIRD societies. And that there has been an assumption that there is little variation across other human cultures and populations.

However, the data available shows a great deal of variation in how test subjects from non-WEIRD cultures think about the world. The most interesting finding is that people from WEIRD cultures, like us, are actually particularly unusual among truly representative samples.

We are "frequent outliers."[38] And yet, the vast majority of psychological research has been performed on us, the least representative group. The areas of significant measured differences are vast, including fairness, cooperation, moral reasoning, self-concepts, reasoning styles, and even visual perception. Their conclusions are summarized as follows:

> *The findings suggest that members of WEIRD societies, including young children, are among the least representative populations one could find for generalizing about humans...Overall, these empirical patterns suggests that we need to be less cavalier in addressing questions of human nature on the basis of data drawn from this particularly thin, and rather unusual, slice of humanity.[39]*

This is a fascinating claim to consider—that we are the outlier among the history of the world, not the norm.

---

38 Ibid
39 Ibid

WEIRD AND NON-WEIRD MORALITY

In *The Righteous Mind*, Haidt discusses this research and draws these conclusions:

> *"The WEIRDer you are, the more you see a world full of separate objects, rather than relationships. It has long been reported that Westerners have a more independent and autonomous conception of the self than do East Asians. For example, when asked to write twenty statements beginning with the words 'I am...,' Americans are likely to list their own internal psychological characteristics (happy, outgoing, interested in jazz), where East Asians are more likely to list their roles and relationships (a son, a husband, an employee of Fujitsu)...*
>
> *If WEIRD and non-WEIRD people think differently and see the world differently, then it stands to reason they would have different moral concerns. If you see a world full of individuals, then you'll want...a morality that protects those individuals and their individual rights. You'll emphasize concerns about harm and fairness.*
>
> *But if you live in a non-WEIRD society in which people are far more likely to see relationships, contexts, groups, and institutions, then you won't be so focused on protecting individuals. You'll have a more sociocentric morality, which means...that you place the needs of groups and institutions first, often ahead of the needs of individuals. If you do that, then a morality based on concerns about harm and fairness won't be sufficient. You'll have additional concerns, and you'll need additional virtues to bind people together."*[40]

WHEN YOU CELEBRATE PLURALISM BUT DON'T REFLECT IT

Secular American culture claims and celebrates the ideas of pluralism, that there isn't one right religion or one way of doing things. Ideals of tolerance, diversity of thought, and multiculturalism are heralded in many capacities. But a romanticized view of pluralism is very difficult to apply consistently when it comes to matters of right and wrong.

---

40 Jonathan Haidt, *The Righteous Mind*, pages 113-114.

In a section of Haidt's book called "How I Became a Pluralist," he chronicles his thought journey, from being a twenty-nine year old atheist with clear liberal views about right and wrong tasked with studying the morality of differing cultures and the changes that would produce in his thinking.

He told of a research trip to India where he experienced some jarring transitions. At first, he was very uncomfortable with the socially stratified and starkly different nature of India, where he dined with men while wives served silently, he was told to stop thanking the servants so much, and everyone seemed devoutly religious. After a few weeks there, his tension faded to a degree and something strange happened: he started to understand them and even like the people. He still saw the weaknesses and potentials for injustice and maltreatment, but he saw more positives than at first:

> *"Rather than automatically rejecting the men as sexist oppressors and pitying the women, children, and servants as helpless victims, I began to see a moral world in which families, not individuals, are the basic unit of society, and the members of each extended family (including its servants) are intensely interdependent. In this world, equality and personal autonomy were not sacred values. Honoring elders, gods, and guests, protecting subordinates, and fulfilling one's role-based duties were more important...*
>
> *I could see beauty in a moral code that emphasizes duty, respect for one's elders, service to the group, and negation of the self's desires. I could still see its ugly side: I could see that power sometimes leads to pomposity and abuse...But for the first time in my life, I was able to step outside of my home morality, the ethic of autonomy. I had a place to stand, and from the vantage point of the ethic of community, the ethic of autonomy now seemed overly individualistic and self-focused...when I boarded the plane to fly back to Chicago I heard a loud voice with an unmistakably American accent saying 'Look, you tell him that this is the compartment over my seat, and I have a right to use it.' I cringed."[41]*

He goes on to talk about gaining positive feelings towards the non-WEIRD ethic of divinity as well, seeing beauty "in a moral code that emphasizes self-control, resistance to temptation, cultivation of one's higher, nobler self, and negation of the self's desires."[42]

---

41 Ibid, p. 119-120
42 Ibid, p.124

This is certainly not to argue that India is a perfect picture of God's Kingdom on Earth—the issues there are not hard for us to see. But this cultural insight causes us to stop and realize that secular American culture isn't necessarily the ideal picture of God's Kingdom either. We have blind spots and weaknesses like other cultures, they are just different. Because each culture has crafted its own unique concoction of moral categories that are stamped deep in our God-given consciences.

Maybe, when zoomed out in view of human history, we actually *are* anomalies.

Maybe, at least to a degree, we are a historical echo chamber. One that happens to be bent to the extremes of individual autonomy—causing us to be so consumed with the issue of harm that we feel totally comfortable rejecting God on its basis.

Maybe that helps explain some of the particular trends we are seeing, the growing allure of deconstruction and de-conversion.

Perhaps the "kingdom without the King" our culture is in search of is deeply deformed in ways we can't easily see, and not at all leading to the flourishing we thought it would bring.

All those interesting questions aside, what we know for a fact is that what the world needs most is not the benefits that come with a wealthy Western democracy, but the culture-spanning wisdom of God and the gospel of Jesus.

CHAPTER 4
YOU SHALL HAVE NO OTHER GODS BEFORE ME

And God spoke all these words, saying, ₂ "I am the Lord your God, who brought you out of the land of Egypt, out of the house of slavery.

₃ You shall have no other gods before me."

Exodus 20:1-3

GOD ON THE MOUNTAIN

In our cultural context, if someone were to remark about another and say "He or she came down from the mountain" to declare some truth, that would be looked upon with eye-rolls or derision. Due to our Enlightenment lineage, we are prone to be suspicious or, tear down, and revolt against authority at almost every level. We tend to think authority is likely evil and exploitative as a default, rather than beneficial. And we especially don't like it when someone seen to be equal with us makes such a mountain-descending claim.

All of this makes the immediate context of the Ten Commandments worth paying close attention. In Exodus 19, as God prepares Moses to get the people ready to hear the Ten Commandments, He goes about it in a way that may seem curious to some today. He does not arrange a listening session or a focus group, or other modern practices we might see a leader do in our context. Rather, He tells Moses to make the people consecrate themselves for three days, cleanse themselves, remain sexually pure, wash their clothes, and prepare to approach the mountain but do not touch it, lest they die.

Because from that mountain, He would speak.

> *On the morning of the third day there were thunders and lightnings and a thick cloud on the mountain and a very loud trumpet blast, so that all the people in the camp trembled. ₁₇ Then Moses brought the people out of the camp to meet God, and they took their stand at the foot of the mountain. ₁₈ Now Mount Sinai was wrapped in smoke because the Lord had descended on it in fire. The smoke of it went up like the smoke of a kiln, and the whole mountain trembled greatly. ₁₉ And as the sound of the trumpet grew louder and louder, Moses spoke, and God answered him in thunder. ₂₀ The Lord came down on Mount Sinai, to the top of the mountain. And the Lord called Moses to the top of the mountain, and Moses went up.*

Exodus 19:16-20

The words of God boomed over the trembling people, rattling their bodies and souls so much so that when God finished speaking, the people were afraid and stood far off, asking Moses to be an intermediary: "You speak to us, and we will listen; but do not let God speak to us, lest we die" (Exodus 20:19). Moses responds by telling them not to cower from Him in fear, but to know that God wants to keep them from sin. As he reminds the people later in Deuteronomy, God let them hear His voice out of heaven and see His great fire "that he might discipline you" (Deuteronomy 4:35-36).

God gathered His redeemed son, Israel, to His feet after their prodigal wanderings not with a coddled, fuzzy appeal, but with the force and weight of life-and-death matters. His voice boomed, made them shake and tremble, not because He is a mean or scary God, but because He loved them and wanted their good. So much so that He starts His address by reminding them of who He is and what He's done for them—He rescued them from slavery. Their obedience to what followed would overflow from His preceding grace, not be a means of earning it.

And then in the first imperative spoken from the mountain, the brute force of the directive fits the setting well.

NO OTHER GODS BEFORE ME

God's dream for the world was for magnificent, created image bearers to live in reality, remaining loyal to Him and under His authority because that was the only way to human flourishing. Eden, which some scholars say originally meant something like "pleasure" or "delight" was dependent upon created beings acting like they were in fact created—their worship of the Creator was the only act capable of sustaining the joy they were designed for. That design was derailed by the temptation of a rival god, the great enemy that spans the pages of Scripture and suffers final defeat at the end.

So God starts with what went wrong in the first place. To live in His house, as His son or daughter, requires His supremacy. The idea that God alone is in charge is the foundation for all other commandments. His supremacy is the starting point for what follows.

God is God, you are not.

God is God, rival gods are not.

God is God, pleasure is not.

God is God, feelings are not.

God is God, freedom is not.

This means He is in charge.

He makes the rules.

He determines right from wrong.

No other entity is capable of any of His unique responsibilities.

He will not compete with any other God, because there is no competition.

In his book, *The Ten Commandments*, Kevin DeYoung explains it this way: "*The God of the Bible is not simply interested in being recognized as a strong and mighty deity. That would not have been a controversial claim in the ancient world. Lots of peoples had lots of impressive gods and goddesses. What was controversial, and what set the Israelites apart from the other nations, was that their God demanded to be worshiped alone, as the only God, to the exclusion of all others...*"

Here's why all of this is so important: the only way for us to perfectly flourish is to have an all-powerful, all-good authority over us that we submit to in all things. Everything that's wrong with the world starts by rejecting this.

God's supremacy is for our good.

IDOLATRY & FREEDOM

The first command is a no-holds-barred claim over reality itself, where this fire-cloaked God dictates what is acceptable and not acceptable, good and evil, and even what is freedom and what is *not* freedom.

This forces us to stop and provide clarity on a topic that culturally can be confusing. Pastor and author John Mark Comer from Portland argues that there is a very important clarification between what the Bible calls freedom and how our culture defaults to think about freedom. Which can lead to confusion when we come across the word "freedom" in Scripture and place our current connotations onto it. The differences are marked by the difference between "freedom from" and "freedom to."

Biblical Understanding	Cultural Understanding of Secularism
Freedom *From*	Freedom *To*
Sin and idolatry enslave us, God frees us *from* our fleshly desires.	Rules and constraints enslave us, we free ourselves *to* chase whatever we want.
Background: Judeo-Christian worldview.	Background: post-Enlightenment worldview.
God is holy and wise.	God is unnecessary, restrictive or oppressive.
Human nature is sinful and needs redemption.	Human nature is inherently good and needs to throw off constraints of any kind.

This is quite an essential difference to understand when considering everything at play here. The Bible claims that sonship in God's family is where we are free, while the world says pursuit of idolatry is where we are free. Scripture doggedly asserts that we are free only within the loving boundaries made for freedom, while culture insists on absolute negative freedom—no restrictions whatsoever.

"What the Bible calls freedom, the world calls slavery, and what the Bible calls slavery the world calls freedom."

John Mark Comer

This means that an increasingly post-Christian culture would hear the first commandment as an inherently enslaving concept. As an external restriction being forced upon humans to keep us from being who we were made to be.

This is incredibly sad, because it misses a primary point of Scripture found from first pages to last.

God was bringing Israel *out* of slavery, not *into* it. He was rescuing them from the horrors of foreign, false gods and the brutality it caused in their lives.

God is not trying to keep you from becoming who you were made to be... He's trying to free you to become who you were made to be!

That mountain trembled for our good.

WHEN YOU BECOME WHO YOU ARE

There is no such thing as absolute freedom in the world God created. An acorn is not free to become an elephant, and a created image bearer is not free to become Creator, King, or Judge.[43] They can certainly try, through the pursuit of lesser gods—primarily the false god of self and its effects of self-rule and self-reliance. But when you worship something it requires sacrifices, and the self is no exception. Self-worship demands the sacrifices and co-idols of status, money, appearance, power, and a thousand others.

But the Bible says that these rival gods always deceive and lie to us. They never deliver the freedom they promise, but instead deform us. We begin to reflect their paltry, pathetic images rather than the glorious image of God. As Psalm 115 ominously warns, those who fashion them become like them.

If you have ever interacted with a profoundly unhealthy person whose spirit and demeanor are overwhelmingly unattractive, and you couldn't pinpoint why but you just wanted to get away from them, this explains why. They have become like what they worship. Their souls have shrunken to the size of the object they worship, a truth that can also be seen in the horror of addiction.

The sad irony is: those who chase idols often think they are *free*.

---

43 Peter Leithart, *The Ten Commandments.*

"Idols are stupid and make us stupid. They make their worshipers as dead as they are."

Peter Leithart, *The Ten Commandments*

God intended to free Israel from the deadening, deforming effect idols have on us, and that is the starting point for His instruction to them. He wanted them to become who they truly are, to come alive with splendor and radiance, as they worship the One their souls were designed for. This would only come through complete submission and non-competitive worship. The earthquake, fire and smoke were not intended to scare would-be subjects into mindless submission, but to bring spiritually deformed children back to the wholeness they were made for. It was a thunderclap call to be who they were, not who they believed themselves to be.

He wants the same for us. He intends for us to become fully human and thrive as His adopted children within the gracious boundaries He has set up for flourishing. It would be foolish to deconstruct them.

> *"And the Lord heard your words, when you spoke to me. And the Lord said to me, 'I have heard the words of this people, which they have spoken to you. They are right in all that they have spoken. 29 Oh that they had such a heart as this always, to fear me and to keep all my commandments, that it might go well with them and with their descendants forever!*
>
> **Deuteronomy 5:28-29**

What a beautiful and blatant echo of "for our good always."

IDOLATRY & BETRAYAL

Commentators note that in the original Hebrew, "You shall have no other gods before me" can also be translated as "You shall bring no other gods before my face," pointing at the intense relational dynamic of rebellion against God.

We are all hardwired with a sense of loyalty. But that sense of loyalty gets prioritized differently in various people and contexts—whether it is loyalty to a family of origin, a nation, a political party, a friend, a group, a leader, etc. The differences come in deciding who should get our loyalty and why, as well as what situations constitute a sufficient reason to betray that loyalty. One example of these differences is looking at views of marriage.

In the relatively low-loyalty West, we have a widespread no-fault divorce ideology where "falling out of love" is a perfectly sufficient reason to break a marital covenant. That stands in stark contrast to communal and duty-based cultures that exist in other parts of the world where divorce is not taken so lightly.

The first commandment answers the foundational question about where our loyalty as created beings should reside: first and always with the God who made us. Reformer John Calvin remarked on the first commandment by saying that the portrayal of sin here is "like a shameless woman who brings in an adulterer before her husband's very eyes, only to vex his mind the more."[44]

Idolatry is always bringing other lovers, or rival gods, before God's face. In the Old Testament it was often foreign gods like Asherah, Baal, or Molech. People would worship Yahweh, and also build a high place for Baal to cover their bases, just in case Baal was real and angry at them, threatening to make their life worse. The problem is that *and*, because when it comes to matters of worship, the God on the Mountain doesn't do *ands*. He will not share His rightful admiration and affection with pretend gods who don't exist, and He will not stand for the deforming effect worship of false gods has on those who bear His likeness.

We might not build high places to worship Asherah anymore, but idolatrous betrayal beckons us still. The siren calls of rival gods whisper to us everywhere, lying to our faces, telling us we can worship:

Yahweh *and* freedom.

Yahweh *and* unrestrained sexual expression.

Yahweh *and* money.

Yahweh *and* fill-in-your-blank.

But the Garden of Eden tells the truth: God does not tolerate devotion to rival gods, and flourishing is destroyed by them.

TREMBLING BEFORE OTHER GODS

In our specific context of an increasingly post-Christian culture, there is a particular rival god we will have to resist: the idol of cultural affirmation.

---

44 John Calvin, *Institutes of the Christian Religion*.

Instead of bowing in reverence before the one true God of history, we are tempted to tremble before the small gods of our cultural moment. We fear that they will sneer at our orthodoxy, judge us backwards or behind-the-times.

Will we humbly trust God alone as wise ruler, remain loyal to Him through tension, hardship, or shifting winds of cultural change? Or will we run up the mountain, usurp God, and insist on changing what He says, all so we can say we worship Yahweh still but have the idol of social respect in our hands?

It's important to note what is happening in the midst of this pressure we face to tremble before lesser gods of culture. Instead of remaining God's "called out ones"—holy and set apart under His reign, enduring the hard for the ultimate good—this is the opposite. It is not easy if others speak evil of you for trusting and submitting to Jesus, no one is suggesting that. But giving into this pressures helps no one. Not you, because in doing so you are tearing down God's authority, betraying His love for you, bringing an idol before His face that cannot remain in His presence. None of which will end up for your good.

And it doesn't help others either, because it dilutes God into eventual nothingness. If He is a god you can bend and mold to your liking to be sure He doesn't dictate anything hard or embarrassing, then what you have in your hands is a paper mache god. Feel free to put this non-god on your shelf if you want. He can speak his silent blessing over you as you chase *your* version of freedom, but he can't save anyone or anything. His affirmation will be empty, void of any substance—and his dictates will lead you out of the Garden, not back into it.

INTERLUDE 4
THE END RESULT OF SECULARISM

"Liberal order is a conspiracy to guard public life from God's intrusions. We strip the town square, then genuflect to the nothing."

Peter Leithart, *The Ten Commandments*

From our historical vantage point, it can be difficult to remember that democracy is an idea. An idea that is fairly new in the span of human life, and is still in the process of being tested. We would argue that it's likely a good idea, one to be continually improved, and none of us are chomping at the bit to live in a different form of government.

Political theory is an important consideration for how to order a society, and one that Christians should thoughtfully participate in with discernment, knowing that our true allegiance will always be to God's kingdom and never to a flag. Because we do not live in a theocracy, it will always be challenging to figure out how to live in a secular culture and advocate for the spiritual and eternal good of people who do not share the same beliefs.

That important discussion is not the focus of this book, however. What we are trying to highlight here is, what are the potential spiritual effects of our particular political ideology? How do the unseen thought processes that came before us and laid the foundation for the world we inhabit have an effect on us that we might not see?

What happens when you make an idol out of freedom and choice?

In a society built on the foundation of liberalism, or "freedomism," the freedoms of autonomous individuals take precedence over other concerns. There are many benefits that come from this, but as with anything there is an underbelly as well.

In this worldview, any restriction of uninhibited freedom feels like suffering. So individuals here seek to be freed from external constraints of community or duty to anything outside of themselves.

University of Notre Dame professor Patrick Deenan, in his book *Why Liberalism Failed*, captured the shift that occurred with this post-Enlightenment political philosophy. He insightfully points out the changes in thought about created order and human nature that occured with John Locke and other Enlightenment thinkers, and notes that the formation of liberalism was the "switch" that flipped *freedom from* to become *freedom to.*

> *"Liberalism rejects the ancient conception of liberty as the learned capacity of human beings to conquer the slavish pursuit of base and hedonistic desires. This kind of liberty is a condition of self-governance of both city and soul, drawing closely together the individual cultivation and practice of virtue ... A central preoccupation of such societies becomes the comprehensive formation and education of individuals and citizens in the art and virtue of self-rule. Liberalism instead understands liberty as the condition in which one can act freely within the sphere unconstrained by positive law."*[45]

Whereas premodern political thought accepted limitations and commitments as necessary for flourishing, liberalism rejected them as oppressive. There are many insights that could be drawn from his arguments about how our underlying philosophy affects us, but just to name a few:

1. **A redefinition of freedom.** Freedom changes from the ancient, biblical conception of boundaries for flourishing to the newer idea of absence of any restraint (absolute negative freedom).

2. **A reactionary spirit.** If you remember back to the Western Secular Liberalism video, this movement downward toward the individual is apparent. Once the train of revolution starts, it can be difficult to know where to stop.

3. **An ironically increasing state.** Deenan remarks that, rather ironically, as the rights and liberties of individuals expand and swell in importance, taking precedence over other concerns—the state has

---

45 Patrick J. Deenan, *Why Liberalism Failed.*

to grow larger and larger to protect those rights. To the point that some legal scholars argue that the United States now has so many laws that no one knows how many there truly are, and Harvard professor Harvey Silverglate estimates that the average American professional unknowingly commits 3 felonies per day.[46]

4. **Loose connections.** Simply put: when freedomism is your ultimate guiding concern, you aren't committed to anything or anyone other than yourself. Freedom at all costs actually requires liberation from all forms of associations and relationships that would exert control over behavior: from family to church to wider community—and even to God. Individual self-interest reigns over any other concern.

In all of this, Deenan is not advocating for a return to some form of dictatorship or monarchy, or for some second revolution. Rather, he is pointing out the weaknesses of our political history and philosophy that occur alongside its many strengths. And it does not take a seminary degree to consider how all of this affects us spiritually as people living in modern America. It turns out Disney wasn't the originator of the call to be "true to yourself above all," but just one prominent later voice calling us to divorce from any commitment or constraint.

Deenan's most scathing critique comes in what liberalism tends to produce:

"Ironically, but perhaps not coincidentally, the political project of liberalism is shaping us into the creatures of its prehistorical fantasy, which in fact required the combined massive apparatus of the modern state, economy, education system, and science and technology to make us into: **increasingly separate, autonomous, nonrelational selves replete with rights and defined by our liberty, but insecure, powerless, afraid, and alone...** *It has remade the world in its image... aimed at achieving supreme and complete freedom through the liberation of the individual from particular places, relationships, memberships, and even identities—unless they have been chosen, are worn lightly, and can be revised or abandoned at will."*[47]

---

46 *Three Felonies a Day: How the Feds Target the Innocent* by Harvey A. Silvergate.
47 Patrick J. Deenan, *Why Liberalism Failed.* Emphasis added.

A METAPHOR FOR UNDERSTANDING

Studies like this are insightful, poking, prodding, but can also be difficult to wrap our minds around. All of this, after all, is not only the air we breathe but the air our ancestors breathed. As previously mentioned, it can feel a bit like you are a fish noticing water for the first time.

Australian political philosopher Kennth Minogue, in his book *A Liberal Mind*, offered a metaphor. He said liberal philosophy is not unlike the old legend of St. George having to slay a dragon to save a princess. He noted that the first dragons slayed by the proverbial St. George of liberalism was "despotic kings" and "religious intolerance," railing his sword against threats to freedom. Then he moved on to dragons of its own making, like slavery and treatment of the poor. Over time, he to varying degrees succeeded in his quest to overcome the dragons of injustice and mistreatment, seeking to create a world without dragons at all. He finishes the metaphor with a statement on the mindset such a motivation can produce:

> *"But, unlike St. George, he did not know when to retire. The more he succeeded, the more he became bewitched with the thought of a world free of dragons, and the less capable he became of ever returning to private life. He needed his dragons...As an ageing warrior, he grew breathless in his pursuit of smaller and smaller dragons—for the big dragons were now harder to come by."*

To be clear: there are still dragons to fight in our culture. There are modern day injustices and effects of historical oppression that are alive and well, and have a disproportionate effect on minorities—most severely on African Americans in our country. Christians should care about these issues and fight for them, as we have always taught.

The use of this metaphor is simply to bring light to a broader cultural reality: just because there are still real dragons does not mean every dragon someone points to is real. In such a historical story and setting, it would make all the sense in the world for people to need their dragons—to search for oppression even where it doesn't exist, and revolt against it.

We now live in a world where biological gender is a dragon, and that is said with the utmost care and concern for those who suffer with gender dysphoria. Up until this point in history, biological gender has been a limitation of reality that must be accepted for psychological health. Now, increasingly so, it functions as a dragon that threatens oppression and must be overthrown by any means necessary.

Our secular authorities in psychology and medicine are lining up to affirm that it is indeed a dragon that needs to be slayed in the name of preventing "harm." Hormone treatments and reassignment surgeries are considered for young children, even though the longest study of post-surgery suicide rates in Sweden, a country very affirming of gender transitions, reports that a transitioned person is up to 20 times more likely to commit suicide than comparable peers.[48]

It is increasingly easy to craft a dragon in our cultural moment. All you have to do is point to how it is harming someone, without considering other essential factors, and soon the public will be convinced that it must be slayed. Hardly anyone stops to consider the tremendous long-term personal and societal damage such actions cause, and if you raise these questions in medicine or academia you may get fired.[49]

The spirit of liberalism can lead to a never-ending search for oppression. In this excessive and sometimes subconscious search, accusations get leveled at any outside constraint or authority figure. People go dragon-hunting everywhere, from the home to the church to the college campus:

- Sinful children rail against an imperfect but sufficient parent's authority.

- Healthy churches who call people to God's authority through clear biblical teachings get accused of being too harsh, legalistic, or even spiritually abusive.[50]

- College students demand protection from speech or ideas that, while far from discriminatory or hate speech, still make them feel unsafe.[51]

---

48 "Long-Term Follow-Up of Transsexual Persons Undergoing Sex Reassignment Surgery: Cohort Study in Sweden" https://journals.plos.org/plosone/article?id=10.1371/journal.pone.0016885
49 "Gender Dissenter Gets Fired" https://www.nationalreview.com/2019/07/allen-josephson-gen-der-dissenter-gets-fired/
50 To be clear, there are absolutely churches and leaders who abuse, manipulate and commit crimes against the people in their churches. These leaders and churches should be held to account, rebuked and prosecuted when applicable. Here however, we have in view the changes in our culture that can lead to everything being called abuse, even healthy biblical actions.
51 For more on the culture of "safetyism," refer to the book *The Coddling of the American Mind*

If people need dragons, dragons will be found. And sadly, within this subconscious mindset, God is in more danger of becoming a dragon than anyone.

But it's worth asking: where does all of this sword swinging leave us? Is it possible the answer is found in what Deenan suggested? That we would be left as: *"increasingly separate, autonomous, nonrelational selves replete with rights and defined by our liberty, but insecure, powerless, afraid, and alone."*

At the very least, we need to be aware of our dragon-hunting lineage—and be mindful of the possibility that we might become a bunch of St. Georges isolated in our own castles, swinging our swords at thin air.

CHAPTER 5

YOU SHALL NOT MAKE FOR YOURSELF A CARVED IMAGE

SANCTITY LOYALTY

You shall not make for yourself a carved image, or any likeness of anything that is in heaven above, or that is in the earth beneath, or that is in the water under the earth. ₅ You shall not bow down to them or serve them, for I the Lord your God am a jealous God, visiting the iniquity of the fathers on the children to the third and the fourth generation of those who hate me, ₆ but showing steadfast love to thousands of those who love me and keep my commandments.

Exodus 20:4-6

NO STUMBLE FROM THE STARTING GATE

The Ten Commandments work as a cohesive whole, a list of family rules for those who would live in God's house. The first commandment starts off with quite a bang. It roars like a thunderclap, demanding attention and daring any who would disagree. After such a start, curiosity might compel one to wonder what would follow on its heels?

And to a secular culture far removed from its context, what comes next may cause some confusion. *Carved images? A jealous God? Iniquity that lasts for generations?*

This is not what some would expect. Oprah is just one such case, who famously said she rejected the God of the Bible because it says He is a jealous God, and jealousy is thought of as pettiness. Off the cuff, this commandment may feel to you like a) I would never do that anyway, b) I'm not entirely sure why such a thing would make a list this important, and c) the potential punishment mentioned seems a little severe.

As is generally the case, context matters a lot for matters like these, and it's not remotely that simple. You may be more implicated than you think.

CREATED TO RULE DOWN & WORSHIP UP

In the creation narrative of Genesis 1, God speaks the realities we now know as the known universe into existence, leading to living, animate creatures that fly in the air, roam the Earth, and swim in the foaming seas. On the sixth day, He fashions the crown jewel of His work.

> *Then God said, "Let us make man in our image, after our likeness. And let them have dominion over the fish of the sea and over the birds of the heavens and over the livestock and over all the earth and over every creeping thing that creeps on the earth."*
>
> *27 So God created man in his own image, in the image of God he created him; male and female he created them.*

Genesis 1:26-27

These creatures were the crescendo of His symphony, forming a sort of mirror image of God Himself. They were made with such dignity and care that God would a few verses later retire the "it was good" spoken over the rest of creation for "it was very good." Only these special image bearers receive this blessing. It hints at the picture of a parent/child relationship, where the likeness is obvious, and both faces light with the glory and joy of the other.

Their purpose is clear: they would have *dominion*, or rule, over the other created things: the fish of the sea, birds of the heavens, livestock of the earth. They would harness the natural resources God planted to expand the Garden outward and cultivate a civilization.

The key to creation-wide flourishing was operating from a clear hierarchy of ordered creation, starting with God at the top, followed by His image-bearing co-rulers, down to animals and other created things.

The place for image bearers in the created order was to rule down, and worship up. Their hands busy with the ordering of creation, their eyes and hearts fixed above on God—so their faces would glow with the "very good" of their Father.

In fact, God repeats this calling for them to exercise dominion over the rest of creation twice in Genesis 1:26-28, reiterating its importance.

What all of this tells us is that in order for God's world, and His creatures, to operate correctly—respecting and following created order is necessary. We worship, trust, and serve God—our faces alight with Him—and we rule over, control with our hands, and shape creation.

Worship up, rule down.

Sin and idolatry reversed this design. We sought to worship down and rule up. Rebellion caused us to serve and trust created things, and seek to have dominion over God. So fitting with the theme, this command is a re-assertion of God's design. It is going back to point at one of the first house rules posted on the wall. In God's house, you sit where your place is—not at the head, but not on the porch either.

This can be summed up like this: *Don't seek to rule over who you were meant to bow to, and don't bow down to what you were meant to rule over.*

DON'T SEEK TO RULE OVER WHO YOU WERE MEANT TO BOW TO

Among the many facets about idolatry that could be teased out of this command, a primary one in context is that *you will not turn God into something you have dominion over.* You will not take God, who is above you, and seek to place Him below you by forcing Him into an image of something that you do have control over.

In other words: God made you with *His* hands—you will not fashion or control Him with *yours*.

Ancient people groups did this in a way that is mostly unfamiliar to us. They would literally fashion an idol out of created materials and serve it as if it were, or at least represented, a god. Most scholars argue that these ancient people weren't dumb: they didn't think the idols were actually gods and goddesses. Rather, they performed rituals to "quicken" the divine essence in the statue.[52]

---

52 Peter Leithart, *The Ten Commandments.*

Yahweh calls Israel out of the common practice of the world around them. He declares that He, the true God, would not be worshipped with graven images crafted to quicken or manipulate His presence. They would not worship the same way their neighbors did, and the reverence and uniqueness they reserved for God would set them apart from all watching eyes.

Sadly this is not what always happened, as Israel descended into cultural forms of worship time and time again. One such occasion was in Exodus 32, when Moses was meeting with God on the mountain. The people grew tired because they did not know where Moses was, or when he was coming back, so they pleaded with Aaron to "make us gods who shall go before us." They pooled together their gold and formed the golden calf.

> And they said, "These are your gods, O Israel, who brought you up out of the land of Egypt!" *5* When Aaron saw this, he built an altar before it. And Aaron made a proclamation and said, "Tomorrow shall be a feast to the Lord." *6* And they rose up early the next day and offered burnt offerings and brought peace offerings. And the people sat down to eat and drink and rose up to play.

Exodus 32:4-5

Their motives, arguably, were at least partially to honor and worship the deity who had rescued them from slavery. Aaron attributes the feast day to the Lord. So it's possible this was not a complete rejection of the God who had revealed Himself to them, but it was a complete rejection of worshipping Him the way He commanded.

God's anger boils at them for doing so, and the righteous jealousy we see mentioned in the second commandment grows evident. Though Father is the most prominent metaphor for God through Scripture, Husband is another, and this may be a more apt picture to describe God's jealousy. He reacts with understandable outrage when He sees the wayward bride, called to Himself through the crinkling pages of Scripture, get into adulterous relationships.

Their mistake was far more grievous than modern minds have the categories to understand, precisely because of the nature of God's holiness and "otherness." We need the lost language of sanctity to understand this about God, because it tells us that holiness is not a cultural or religious construct, but a reality. God sits atop the order of all created things as completely "other" than the rest, holy and set apart, unlike anything or anyone else. He is indefinable, irreducible, and He will not be toyed with or molded by those He created.

"Degradation" is the act of treating someone or something in lower, or more base ways than they are designed to be treated. When you treat a human being in inhumane ways, you degrade them. Likewise, any act of making God seem smaller than He is in reality is guilty of the same thing.

The reality we find in Scripture is that God defines us, we do not define Him. God marks out our boundaries and edges, we do not mark out His. God encapsulates us in His image, we do not seek to encapsulate Him in an image.

So our attempts to control or manipulate God by putting Him in the confines of something we can manage, even if done with the pretense of "worship," will not be tolerated.

We will not rule over He who we are meant to bow to. While most of us don't fashion golden forms to worship, there is no shortage of hand-crafted gods to choose from in the pantheon of secularism:

The rush of profit and the sacrifices it demands.

The allure of approval.

The freedom to do as we please.

The pleasure of unboundaried sex.

We are increasingly tempted to fashion a wrathless god who doesn't disagree with us about anything important. A god whom culture might accept, because he is just as afraid of offending someone as we often are. We knock off all the hard edges so we land on a smooth idol that no one will have a problem so that we can stay in the good graces of the world we were called to stand apart from and hold out hope to.

No matter the particular form, God will not be ruled by those who can't even breathe without His ongoing assistance. And one day, every knee will bow, in heaven and on Earth, when everything is put back right again (Phil 2:10).

DON'T BOW DOWN TO WHAT YOU WERE MEANT TO RULE OVER

The other side of the logical coin found in this command reflects back to Genesis 1. It repudiates a picture of a human image bearer bowing down to serve and worship an image of a created thing. After the primary concern of offending God's glory and holiness, it begs a question:

What are you doing, *human*?

Why are *you* bowing down, to *that*? You were meant to rule *over* that.

And therein lies the truth: that idolatry is not only a stench in God's righteously jealous nostrils, it's also degrading to the humans who participate in it.

It's...embarrassing.

Beneath our created dignity.

Ironically sad.

The truth is, God has a higher view of humanity than you do.

You may be tempted to believe the opposite. That God must want to keep humans down in their place, not let them be fully themselves, not encourage their freedom, autonomy or desires. That's common thought, proof that our cultural view of a human being is basically a glorified animal, whose base appetites must reign.

Meanwhile, God wants you to actually reign. With Him, over creation. As a redeemed son, a ransomed daughter, freed from enslaving desires, uninspired trinkets, and degrading pleasures to become who you were meant to be. He wants to form you into the kind of solidified person who would prefer and enjoy a perfectly ordered, remade creation where all things are in subjection to Him and blossoming with His joy. Not unlike the Bright People from C.S. Lewis' novel *The Great Divorce*, who have grown real enough to live in God's delight, whose feet are strong enough to walk on His grass, and whose arms are capable of picking up an apple whose weight would crush someone on Earth. God's invitation to us is nothing short of an invitation to reality, with all of its hard but glorious edges.

Idolatry, on the other hand, turns you into Gollum from *Lord of the Rings*. Obsessed with your *precious*, sniveling and deformed, pursuing it at any cost. It turns you into a disordered person, profoundly off-kilter but unable to see the disorder—the wrinkled self—in the mirror. It makes you less human while convincing you it's what you need to be fully alive. That's the great deceit and irony in it. And it begs the question:

If everyone around you is also Gollum, how would you ever see it?

Disordered people tend to pass on and replicate their disorder. This explains the punishment hinted at in the commandment, that God would visit iniquity to three or four generations. But there is a key phrase that is often missed: *visiting the iniquity of the fathers on the children to the third and the fourth generation **of those who hate me**, but showing steadfast love to thousands of those who love me and keep my commandments.*

This is not a willy nilly hand-me-down of punishment from God to great-great grandchildren for the sins of their forefathers. Evidently this misunderstanding was common enough that it had to be explained in Ezekiel 18, which says that is not the case, and that "the soul who sins shall die."

> *The soul who sins shall die. The son shall not suffer for the iniquity of the father, nor the father suffer for the iniquity of the son.*

> ### *Ezekiel 18:20*

"Ezekiel will not let us have this view of the second commandment," as Kevin DeYoung says. Rather, God is saying that those who hate God will incur His wrath, and hatred of God seems to be contagious, even through family lines. Deformed humans often raise deformed humans.

And the conclusion to the commandment, juxtaposed with the former warning, cannot be missed: *but showing steadfast love to thousands of those who love me and keep my commandments.*

This is the heart and intention of God—to show steadfast love to hard-to-number crowds, spanning locales and generations, all learning to live and flourish while bowing under His rule. And therefore learning how (and what) to rule over, as remade humans starting to look like God intended.

And of course, through the lineage of the "thousands" came the God-man Jesus. The truly perfect Son from heaven, come to show us what a human was supposed to look like. He walked the Earth for 33 years and never once bucked up to the One above Him, and never bowed down to anyone or anything beneath Him.

His life was marveled at, applauded, remembered, and also hated because He is the only person in history to perfectly bow and rule. He showed us what Adam was supposed to look like, and He was strong enough to stay in that place even though it got Him killed.

And thank God that He did, because His death made a way for serial idolaters, who debase both God and themselves—whose iniquities would have continued to pass down—to be forgiven, cleansed, and adopted into a family where they sit at God's table.

Where He said they belonged, all along.

INTERLUDE 5
HE'S NOT FROM HERE

Your vision's been clouded by this world's delight
But I tell you, you're not of this world, so stand up and fight
You're not of this world, so stand up and fight
There is a peace, to settle your soul
There is a peace and it's calling you home

There is a Peace, by Harvest

A SENTENCE WORTH REMEMBERING

Remarking about the strategy of the devil—the enemy of God and humanity all through Scripture—pastor John Mark Comer makes a helpful argument. This being's purpose is made clear by Jesus in John 10, that his aim is to kill, steal and destroy—to tear down anything that resembles life, joy, and flourishing. But how does he go about seeking to accomplish said destruction? Comer's summary is the following:

*"Satan's primary strategy is **deceitful ideas** that play to **disordered desires** that are normalized in **a sinful society**."*

Taken together, this sentence illustrates the classic understanding of the 3 enemies of the Christian:

The Devil: What does the devil do? He lies, as Jesus teaches in John 8, when He says that he is the father of all lies. But He doesn't go after outlandish lies that are easy to spot. It would do him no good to convince you that Elvis is alive. Rather, he crafts deceitful ideas, ones that might sound or feel true, but in reality are diabolical in nature.

The Flesh: The most effective deceitful ideas are ones that have a hook into particular disordered desires. The ones that get after sin tendencies and weaknesses that we are prone to, that sound appealing to our flesh nature.

"Elvis is alive" has no hook in you. It's empty. On the other hand, "You should get to do whatever makes you happy," well...that one hooks.

The World: All of this strategy is the most effective when administered to a group, convincing a whole society to function on the same lies. When this can happen, the deceit becomes *normalized*—it sinks invisibly into the background, because it's all the people know. Groupthink leads us to believe that normal must = healthy.

This is far easier to see in a culture where their particular outworking of this feels preposterous to you. Consider the golden calf the Israelites formed and made sacrifices to. No one reading this book will likely be tempted to do such a thing. But in their culture, it was incredibly normal. Everyone did it. Not because they were ancient and stupid, but because they thought it was the key to make their lives better, to get the gods of plenty and pleasure to bless them.

Because God loved them, He was not concerned with what was normalized in their culture. He did not turn into some spineless pushover in the sky who said, "Oh well, their entire worldview is based on a lie, but they mean well and are just doing what is normal." Such an attitude would have been evidence of disinterest towards them, not a Father's love (Hebrews 12:7-8).

Instead He forcefully called them out of the normal they inhabited, like a father disciplining his son and saying, "Because I love you, what you are doing will not be normal in my house."

The story of the gospel is that God so loved the world that He sought to make a redeemed son of the world, but in order to do so He had to give the life of His one and only eternal Son (John 3:16). Jesus was our model and sacrifice—the model of the perfect Son, and the sacrifice our sin required to become right with God again.

JESUS WAS NOT NORMAL

When Jesus arrived on Earth, He made it clear through His teaching that His authority stemmed from where He came from.

> *He said to them, "You are from below; I am from above. You are of this world; I am not of this world.*

> **John 8:23**

Jesus emphatically declares, "I am not from here," and that is a bomb that explodes with implications. This explains the seismic impact Jesus had on history, as well as the magnetism He displayed on Earth. People flocked to him, kids huddled around His feet, disciples marveled in amazement at His words and works.

The most famous sermon of Jesus, the Sermon on the Mount, is framed up by Jesus saying "You have heard *this*, but I tell you *that*." Like a messenger from a foreign country, He upends the collected wisdom of the day. This caused some to be cut to the heart by His beauty and truth, and others want to kill Him.

In Mark 4, He even sleeps soundly on a boat rocked by a storm, seemingly unaware that in such a situation it is incredibly normal to freak out. He stops the wind with His voice and asks His disciples, non-rhetorically, why they were so afraid.

They marveled at His abnormalcy.

> *And they were filled with great fear and said to one another, "Who then is this, that even the wind and the sea obey him?"*

> **Mark 4:41**

Their question rings throughout history: *who then is this?* Who *is* this man with wisdom from a higher country, authority over sickness, demons and waves? This man who is unafraid of any ruler, who stands up to evil at any cost to Himself, who can lay down His life and take it back up again?

The answer is that He is who He says He is. The incarnate Son of God, the Second Adam, the firstfruits of a new creation.

He is not from here.

And that means: what's normal to *us* is not normal to *Him*.

He came to tear down what has been normalized here—to destroy the works of the devil (1 John 3:8). And in doing so, to rebuild the humanity and the world that God dreamed of from the beginning. He speaks the truth, however hard to hear it may be, because He *is* the Truth. So it can set us free from slavery to the world, the flesh and the devil.

He calls His *ekklesia*—His "called out ones"—to Himself, and gets them ready to live where He came from.

In chapters 14-17 of John's biography about Jesus, we see a beautiful display of this. Jesus is seeking to prepare His disciples for His death, and the scene is heartfelt and emotional. There are many things He lovingly guides them through in this address, but a primary one is how they would fit into and relate to the world as children of God.

He warns His friends that the world may hate and not accept them, because it first hated Him.

> *"If the world hates you, know that it has hated me before it hated you. 19 If you were of the world, the world would love you as its own; but because you are not of the world, but I chose you out of the world, therefore the world hates you. 20 Remember the word that I said to you: 'A servant is not greater than his master.' If they persecuted me, they will also persecute you.*
>
> **John 15:18-20**

What we know about history makes this scene even more poignant. Early church records indicate that most, if not all of Jesus' disciples sitting around the room that night would be martyred for their joyful and obstinate worship of Jesus in the midst of cultural persecution. These were no empty words, but a lifeline that would sustain them and ring in their ears through unimaginable earthly ends.

They followed Him into the glory of a remade world because He went through death first. Of these beautiful souls, the writer of Hebrews would say that this world "was not worthy of them" (Heb 11:38). They followed Jesus out of the normalized patterns of this world, into the normal of eternity, and their reward for doing so will make their sacrifice feel small in comparison (Rev 21:1-5).

> *I have said these things to you, that in me you may have peace. In the world you will have tribulation. But take heart; I have overcome the world.*
>
> **John 16:33**

WILL WE LIKEWISE FOLLOW?

His words were not just for them, but for us in the downline of history as well. We also find ourselves in a particular culture assaulted by deceitful ideas that play to disordered desires that have been normalized in our sinful society. Our world says lots of things are normal that God forbids:

Change what you don't like about God to suit your needs. Have sex with whomever you want to. Date that unbeliever, because he's really nice after all. Sure, you aren't married yet, but go ahead and move in together— who does that hurt? Don't feel pressure to be generous with your money, you earned it after all...you should enjoy it all. Don't respect the spiritual authority God has placed over you, because authority is rarely ever trustworthy—listen only to the voice inside you.

Jesus meets our culture's distorted desires with piercing questions:

Who told you that was normal?

Who told you you should follow your heart above all else?

Who told you that chasing unboundaried freedom would lead to your joy?

Who told you that God is not for your good?

And so we are pulled between two different worlds—two visions of normalcy—and we must make a choice. We must resist the tides that pull toward the world, and be prophetically suspicious of the things that have been normalized. Knowing that they may be the schemes of the enemy, designed to destroy us without our knowledge.

Jesus stands above and apart. He is not from here, and He invites us to forsake the familiarity of normal for something far, far better. It may come with a cost, but it comes with a much greater reward. It comes with a country not made by men, beautifully unstained by rebellion. A country whose glory is so radiant, martyrs look to it to steel their resolve—forsaking the table of the world for the table of God.

Here we have found no lasting city, so we seek the one that is to come (Heb 13:14). The crumbling city of this world might feel dear to us, but it is filled with empty hopes and false promises.

It does not have the table we were made for.

CHAPTER 6

YOU SHALL NOT TAKE THE NAME OF THE LORD YOUR GOD IN VAIN

You shall not take the name of the Lord your God in vain, for the Lord will not hold him guiltless who takes his name in vain.

Exodus 20:7

A CULTURAL CASE STUDY

In 1989, artist Andres Serrano released a 5 foot tall photography exhibit entitled *Piss Christ*. He suspended a detailed plastic crucifix in a jar of his own urine, and then took a red and yellow photograph of the jar. You can make out the grain of the wood and the outstretched figure of Jesus through the bubbles of urine rising to the surface.

The image has sparked controversy for decades, with some seeking to have it banned from museums, and others defending it as art.[53]

Ten years later, British artist Chris Ofili released a painting he titled *The Holy Virgin of Mary*. The 8 feet tall painting features a depiction of Mary, robed in blue, with one breast uncovered and made from dried and varnished elephant dung. Mary is symbolically surrounded by angels, as in other works of art, but these "angels" are actually representations of human genitalia. The painting itself rests on two large chunks of dried elephant dung, with "Virgin" carved on one and "Mary" on the other.

---

53 The artist, for what it's worth, describes himself as a Christian and encourages viewers to think about the humanity of Jesus, even including bodily functions. "Andres Serrano's controversial Piss Christ goes on view in New York" https://www.theguardian.com/artanddesign/2012/sep/28/andres-serrano-piss-christ-new-york

It sold for 4.6 million dollars, even after a 72 year-old museum visitor smeared white paint all over it.[54]

So...on a scale from 1 to 72 year-old museum visitor, how do you feel about these exhibits? What is your comfort level with them? Do they bother you? Do the museums that hold them feel polluted or degraded to any degree?

Would you decry them as sacrilegious, defend them as art—or somewhere in between?

Now that you have those answers, let's consider a different angle on the question:

Would you feel any different if the figures in question in these exhibits were not Jesus or Mary, but, say...if the image suspended in urine was Martin Luther King, Jr.? Or if the picture covered in elephant poop and genitalia was Rosa Parks?[55]

Would those works produce any difference in reaction for you? What about the wider public? Would those be displayed by museums? If they happened to be, what is the likelihood that people would consider that museum to be tainted and polluted with some invisible evil and degradation?

Obviously, images such as those would be worth the utmost outrage and shunning, because they would degrade image bearers of God and pollute the world with their racism. They would contaminate the world with vile hatred, disrespect, and dehumanization.

So if that is true of image *bearers*, it's worth considering how it applies when directed toward God Himself, the One whose image we are made in.

Regardless of your thoughts about artistic expression, freedom of speech, and other important considerations, this exercise brings up an important question:

What makes you shudder?

What does it take to get a visceral reaction out of you, where you unequivocally point to something and say with your deep intuitions, "That is evil...that is degraded...contaminated...I want no part of that."

---

54 "Chris Ofili's controversial, dung-decorated Virgin Mary painting sold for $4.6 million" https://qz.com/441976/chris-ofilis-controversial-dung-decorated-virgin-mary-painting-sold-for-4-6-million/

55 This exercise in "flipping the politics" is introduced by Jonathan Haidt on p.123 of *The Righteous Mind*, where these examples are discussed.

THE LOST LANGUAGE SURFACES AGAIN

To many modern people, the third commandment may be another curious one. How God is addressed, spoken about, and treated is so important that it makes the famous list, taking up space where others theoretically could have been included.

That is largely explained by what we've already concluded: we are a culture that increasingly has lost sight of the moral foundation of sanctity. Any society where 73% of a college's students can't condemn bestiality on a dead chicken—because something being disgusting doesn't make it wrong—has seen this foundation float out to sea. The same can be said for a culture that lacks the moral fluency to boldly condemn incest without potential harm, or a society where *Fifty Shades of Grey* is a runaway bestseller and box office hit.

The basis of the foundation of sanctity is that some things are "untouchable" on the extremes of a vertical dimension that runs from holiness at the top to degradation at the bottom.

Untouchable Heights: Some things are so holy and elevated and "other" that they are not to be degraded, demeaned, or belittled. They hold such immense power and glory that they are not to be handled with human hands, much like the Ark of the Covenant in the Old Testament. We are meant to tremble with honor and respect for the High Things, and when someone speaks a curse or verbally spits at such a Being or sacred object, that is intended to provoke disgust and horror.

Untouchable Depths: In the opposite direction, some acts are so base and degraded that they cause us to run away from them in repulsion. Different cultures would have varied thoughts on what is worthy of triggering this disgust mechanism, with high divinity cultures having the most categories for this and high autonomy cultures having the least.

The best metaphor to understand the negative side is contagion: that these profane acts are actually spiritually and morally contagious. They risk spreading, contaminating, and implicating others. The disgust and revulsion felt in response to them is what psychologist Mark Schaller calls our "behavioral immune system."[56]

---

56 Jonathan Haidt, *The Righteous Mind*, p.172.

In the physical realm, understanding of this natural impulse to avoid contamination experienced a worldwide revival when the coronavirus pandemic hit: suddenly people were acutely aware that the acts of others could potentially contaminate them, and vice versa.

And that again begs the question posed earlier: what causes that response in you spiritually? What things cause you to move back and away, to avoid spiritual or moral contamination? In a world of anything-goes freedomism (unless it harms someone), how long could our list really be?

Philosopher Leon Kass, in an essay titled "The Wisdom of Repugnance," argued that our receptors to these triggers are often numbed, and they are trying to tell us something if we will only listen:

> *"In this age in which everything is held to be permissible so long as it is freely done, in which our given human nature no longer commands respect, in which our bodies are regarded as mere instruments of our autonomous rational wills, repugnance may be the only voice left that speaks up to defend the central core of our humanity. Shallow are the souls who have forgotten how to shudder."*

What a piercing last line that is: shallow are the souls who have forgotten how to shudder.

Could it be that our greatly reduced cultural sense of sanctity explains any amount of confusion we have over why God would care so much about His name?

THE NAME REVEALED

When you want to get to know a person, you start with their name. Names define and give clarity, providing a shape and outline for who it is you are talking to and what they are like. They carry meaning, as you find when you notice that you feel one way when you hear your favorite person's name, and entirely different when you hear your not-so-favorite person's name.

Names also reveal specificity. Think about the name Tim for example. Which Tim are we talking about? You probably know many Tims. So we come up with different ways of specifying. In the olden days, it might have been Tim of Berkshire. Now it's Tim Smith, or Tim Olson, or Tim Oneal. And if you have more than one Tim Smith, then you go to story or background information: Tim Smith, who grew up in Atlanta and works at the hospital.

To a certain degree, the same thing happens with God in the Old Testament. The first verse in the Bible tells us that in the beginning, God created the heavens and the Earth. But in ancient times, there were thought to be many gods. The Hebrew word used there is Elohim, which is not actually a name, but a title. It's very similar to the English word for God—you as a Christian could use that word and your Hindu neighbor could use that word—but you are not talking about the same God.[57]

So throughout the Old Testament, after our first parents were removed from the Garden for redefining good and evil for themselves, we pick up more information. An old man named Abram hears from God in Genesis 12, promising that He will make a great nation out of him and his barren wife if he will trust and follow Him. Abram is given a new name, Abraham—a stark contrast to the Tower of Babel in Genesis 11 where people tried to make a name for themselves. With this, the nation of Israel is born.

In the book of Exodus we find Israel enslaved to the Egyptians, crying out to God because of their brutal oppression. In chapter 3, Moses is shepherding a flock through the wilderness when he comes upon Mount Horeb, described as the "mountain of God" and widely thought to be another name for Mount Sinai, where the Ten Commandments would later happen.

Moses sees an angel of the Lord in the midst of a bush that is burning continually, but not being consumed. He moves closer to see this spectacle, and God calls to him by name out of the bush. God then warns him not to come any closer, and to take off his shoes, because the place he is standing is holy ground.

God then gives him background information to identify himself—that He is the God of Abraham, Issac, and Jacob. While Moses hides his face from the booming voice emitting from fire, God tells him that he has heard the cries of his people, seen their affliction, and would surely rescue them from the hand of the Egyptians and bring them in to a good land where they would flourish (Exodus 3:1-11).

---

57 For more information on this, see the Bible Project video: Word Study: YHWH - "LORD" https://www.youtube.com/watch?v=eLrGM26pmM0 or the Bible Project podcast Yahweh Is Our God. https://bibleproject.com/podcast/i-am-who-i-am-part-1-yahweh-our-god/

Moses is quite nervous about standing up to Pharoah, and in verse 12 God makes an amazing promise to him:

> *He said, "But I will be with you, and this shall be the sign for you, that I have sent you: when you have brought the people out of Egypt, you shall serve God on this mountain."*

Exodus 3:12

How cool is that? God says, "I will overthrow the evil tyrant, free you from slavery, and then I'll bring you back here to this mountain to serve me." Which is exactly what He had done by the time Moses received the Ten Commandments.

But Moses, understandably anxious about such a task, asks an important question.

> *Then Moses said to God, "If I come to the people of Israel and say to them, 'The God of your fathers has sent me to you,' and they ask me, 'What is his name?' what shall I say to them?"* 14 *God said to Moses, "I am who I am." And he said, "Say this to the people of Israel: 'I am has sent me to you.'"* 15 *God also said to Moses, "Say this to the people of Israel: 'The Lord, the God of your fathers, the God of Abraham, the God of Isaac, and the God of Jacob, has sent me to you.' This is my name forever, and thus I am to be remembered throughout all generations.*

Exodus 3:13-15

THE NAME: DETAILS & IMPLICATIONS

When God reveals His name to Moses, His answer is a variation of the Hebrew verb "to be." It can be translated "I am who I am," "I am what I am," or "I will be what I will be." This is the first time God is not referred to by title or role, but by personal revealed name.

It is translated into English as Yahweh, and anytime your English Bible writes LORD in all capital letters, it is referring to Yahweh, the personal name of Israel's God. (Other times, when not capitalized, it refers to the Hebrew word *adon* which means "lord" or "master" as a role that can also be used to describe kings and people other than God).[58]

---

58 Bible Project: Word Study: YHWH - "LORD" https://www.youtube.com/watch?v=eLrGM26pmM0

In the simplest form, when Moses repeated the name God gave Him to say to the Israelites, it would have sounded to their ears like *"He will be* has sent me to you."* That may sound confusing, but it has profound implications.

There is a limit to which we can understand the nature of God, and even the depths of meaning behind His revealed name. But just as a start, God's revealed name tells us that He will not be named by anyone. Everyone else who has ever existed has been *given* a name. It was externally placed on them, giving shape to their being without any input from the one being named. So God, in effect, is saying *"There is no one before me to give me a name."* As the origination point for all existence, He does not get named, He only names.

We glean from this name that He is eternally self-existent, not in need of anything or anyone. He has always been, and will always be. As far as your mind can go in any direction of time or history or space, He is there, existing without any threat of not existing.

He just, *is*.

This name is a claim over reality itself. He determines what is real and what is not, what is true and what is not, what exists and what doesn't. In the vertical line of things from sacred to profane, He resides alone at the very top. He is so holy—meaning unique, set apart—that even His name communicates how utterly *different* He is from us.

He is not Tim, Sarah, Antoine, Carlos, Susan, Ebony, Moses, or Michelle.

He is *Yahweh*. His name rattles the Earth, holds thunder and lightning and fire in its breath.

GIVING WEIGHT TO THE NAME

Into a culture that has largely forgotten how to shudder, with fewer and smaller spaces for our hard-wired disgust triggers to function as they were designed to, the third commandment is a blaring wake-up call.

Even for Christians who try to take it seriously, it can be seen as more of a wise suggestion rather than a command on the level of "Do not murder." Watch out for what you say, be careful with your OMGs. But is that the extent of what we are called to in this command? Especially when later on in the Old Testament, eye-raising severity would be attached to violating it?

In his book *The Ten Commandments*, Kevin DeYoung brings some helpful clarity: *"If we think violating the third commandment is a light offense, we are quite mistaken. In Leviticus 24:16 we read, 'Whoever blasphemes the name of the Lord shall surely be put to death. All the congregation shall stone him. The sojourner as well as the native, when he blasphemes the Name, shall be put to death.' Granted, this is a civil law for the nation of Israel. The parallel for us would be church discipline, not public execution (1 Cor. 5:9–13). But the Levitical instruction clearly shows us the severity of the sin. Even the sojourner was liable to punishment. Whether you were visiting Israel or native born, it was to be understood that the name of the Lord was holy and not to be blasphemed under any circumstance."*

Even though such a punishment does not apply to us in the New Covenant of grace, it still can get filed under *Things That Make You Go Wow*. It's important to remember, again, that just because something doesn't feel normal to us does not mean it must be wrong. Too often it is we who are wrong, just on the other side of the cliff.

Cursing using the names of God would certainly fall under the category of taking the Lord's name in vain. Granted, modern cursing is a bit different than Old Testament cursing, which was more like intentional blasphemy than a nasty habit. But questions of severity aside—the point is that God's name should not flippantly come out of our mouths. His name should be spoken with great care and respect—not thrown around with other words our culture uses for shock or outrage.[59]

In his book, DeYoung lists other ways we see the command broken in Scripture:

- It forbids empty and false oaths made in the name of God (Lev 19:12).
- It forbids false visions and false claims to speak on God's behalf (Jer 23:25). We are not to prophesy lies in His name or use "God told me" language carelessly.
- Touching the holy things in the tabernacle was considered a violation of this command, because it was not treating them with the sacred attitude they deserved (Lev 22:2)

---

59 Kevin DeYoung, *The Ten Commandments*.

- Strangely enough, sacrificing one's children to the false god of Molech violated this command because it profaned the name of God (Lev 18:21).

The theme we see in all of these examples is the weight and reverence we give the name of God, by the way we speak and act toward what He has declared holy.

WORDS AS FRUIT

Jesus expounds on the weight of our words when He teaches that our speech comes out of the abundance of our hearts (Luke 6:43-45). Good words are the fruit of a heart made good that uses speech to honor, dignify, and lift up. On the other hand, evil words are the fruit of an evil heart, who use speech to tear down or destroy.

The extremes of evil speech can be plainly seen through the abhorrence of hate speech or racial slurs, because those words reveal a heart that degrades and despises image bearers, and has led to unthinkable injustices. Speech like this is a clear way to see the "untouchable depths" of human behavior—something so vile that we should shudder, boldly condemn, and run from the hatred it harbors.

Our speech reveals our inner reality, what we hold high and what we esteem as low.

The same concept applies to God—how we speak about Him reveals our heart toward Him. We can speak about Him in ways that honors His otherness and supremacy, or we can speak about Him in ways that mock or belittle Him.

Obeying this commandment requires attention in secular culture, where common ways of speaking about Him can range from detached indifference to condescending derision. Our culture speaks about God flippantly, and we are called to rebel against that with passion.

The Scriptures are clear, God will not be mocked (Galatians 6:7). To do so is a dangerous path.

Charles Finney, pastor and leader in The Second Great Awakening, warned of these dangers: "To mock God is to pretend to love and serve him when we do not; to act in a false manner, to be insincere and hypocritical in our professions, pretending to obey him, love, serve, and worship him, when we do not. Mocking God grieves the Holy Spirit, and sears the conscience; and thus the bands of sin become stronger and stronger. The heart becomes gradually hardened by such a process."

We have all failed in many ways to give God the proper weight and admiration He deserves with our words and actions, and have no hope of being declared righteous in this command on our own. Our words to and about God have revealed the condition of our hearts that are desperately in need of a Savior.

Thankfully, Jesus stands alone as the only perfect Son, ready and willing to save. Jesus flawlessly honored the glory of His Father, never once disrespecting or belittling His name. Jesus honored the Father's wishes even through excruciating pain because of the perfect love and admiration He had for Him. Through His sacrifice we are adopted by grace—having no business being near God's throne on our own, now able to draw near, covered in the righteousness of another.

And so we learn to be children of Yahweh. We learn to see Him rightly, ever aware of the power and otherness we've been given the right to draw near to, and the grace of being told the Name. To live in His house means we honor, respect, and glorify His name, joining with the cosmos in singing His praises. We bear witness to the untouchable heights seen at the fiery mountain, who calls us to magnify His name for our good.

May we learn to shudder at the thought of not doing so.

INTERLUDE 6

THE ROAD TO EMMAUS: A METAPHOR FOR SECULAR CULTURE

During a lecture at the University of Louvain, Belgian thinker Edward Schillebeeckx (yes that's spelled correctly) was asked if he could think of a biblical story or text that best encapsulates our modern relationship to faith, and he gave a brilliant response: "The disciples walking on the road to Emmaus on Easter Sunday."

The disciples, after the humiliation and bitter disappointment of the crucifixion, had their hopes brutally collapse. Their hope was in Jesus as the Messiah, who would be coronated as King in Jerusalem. Instead, he was killed, the only crown he wore made of thorns.

The story in Luke 24 finds two of them walking away from Jerusalem, God's sacred place of presence, to Emmaus. We are not told why they are going to Emmaus, just that they are walking away. As they are walking, the risen Jesus appears and walks with them, but they do not recognize Him. He asks why they are so discouraged, and they marvel at Him, asking: *"Are you the only visitor to Jerusalem who does not know the things that have happened there in these days?"*[60]

They report that some female disciples had claimed to see Jesus risen from the dead that morning, but that they didn't believe them. The cynicism in their hearts is apparent as Jesus calls them foolish and slow of heart, explaining that if they had listened to Jesus they would have known He was to be crucified. Their hearts burn as he talks, but they still do not recognize Him.

---

60 Luke 24:18

Until that night, when Jesus stays with them for supper. He breaks bread and their eyes are opened in great joy to see He is risen indeed. Jesus vanishes from their presence, and they quickly rush back to Jerusalem with good news and bursting hope.

Remarking on this story in his book *Sacred Fire*, Ronald Rolheiser notes the picture we see of a post-Christian, secular culture in these disciples:

"The situation of today's Christians in our secularized cultures is basically the same: we are walking on the road to Emmaus, discouraged, our youthful faith crucified...They are walking away from Jerusalem toward Emmaus. "Jerusalem," for Luke, represents three things: the faith dream of the disciples, the church, and the place of crucifixion. "Emmaus," on the other hand, represents a place of escape, of worldly consolation. Thus, in symbol, Luke is telling us this: the two disciples in this story are walking away from their faith dream, away from the church, and away from the place where Christ has been humiliated, and they are walking toward a place of human consolation."

That sounds an awful lot like the de-converted, no? It feels eerily similar to the spirit of secularism, which sees the authority and boundaries of Jesus as unthinkable and embarrassing, just as these disciples felt about the crucifixion.

We live in a world that is increasingly *walking away*. One that is sad like they were, aimless and confused like they were, disappointed and disenchanted with life like they were. One walking towards Emmaus, a city without Jesus as King, in hopes of human consolation.

Even while acknowledging that, the story gives us great hope. Why?

Because Jesus didn't let them get to Emmaus.

He instead patiently walked beside them, asked questions, and forcefully contradicted them when necessary. He stayed with them even when they didn't know He was there, following, pursuing, explaining. This is unprovable, but Rolheiser argues that their inability to recognize Him was not necessarily some Jedi mind trick of Jesus, or because His resurrected body looked so different—but explained by their inability to accept Jesus as a humiliated and crucified Savior.

And then He breaks the bread, and their eyes light with the rejoicing of resurrected hope, no longer set on the worldly consolations of Emmaus. They race back to Jerusalem, hearts afire.

What Jesus did for them was integrate the crucifixion into their worldview. It was something they couldn't tolerate, couldn't stomach. Their hopes and personal reputations died with Jesus, as He was nailed to that cross, the most embarrassing and despicable way a human could die at that time. It was the opposite of the glory they expected from a King.

So He graciously explains until they are able to see it: the humility and embarrassment of the cross was necessary for their own resurrection, and for the resurrection of the world.

The hang ups of secularism are different. We don't have as much of a problem with a God who loves us so much He's willing to sacrifice His life for us. That is accepted and beautiful to some degree. But we do have a major problem with that God demanding that we sacrifice our lives for Him, to follow Him no matter if we understand or agree (John 12:23-26). That is the knot in the stomach of a secular world, on the way to our own Emmaus, a city with no King but us.

He walks with us still. He walks with our friends who are walking away. He integrates humility into our worldview, preaching the reality that the cross necessarily comes before the resurrection we desperately need and long for.

That we must leave Emmaus if we want Jerusalem.

CHAPTER 7

OBSERVE THE SABBATH AND KEEP IT HOLY

SANCTITY

Remember the Sabbath day, to keep it holy. ₉ Six days you shall labor, and do all your work, ₁₀ but the seventh day is a Sabbath to the Lord your God. On it you shall not do any work, you, or your son, or your daughter, your male servant, or your female servant, or your livestock, or the sojourner who is within your gates. ₁₁ For in six days the Lord made heaven and earth, the sea, and all that is in them, and rested on the seventh day. Therefore the Lord blessed the Sabbath day and made it holy.

Exodus 20:8-11

"Sabbath is one of the clearest signs of the gospel. You accomplish nothing and God still loves you."

Rich Villodas

THE GOD WHO RESTS

In biblical Hebrew, the language of the Old Testament, the number seven is connected to the idea of fullness or completeness. So it's no surprise that in the creation narrative, God works and creates for the first six days, bringing order and beauty out of chaos and disorder, and then on the seventh He ceases His work. He stops the rhythm of the week, the ups and downs of day and night, for an acknowledgement that His work is complete.[61]

This gives us profound insight into the nature and character of God. In ancient mythology, gods and goddesses were thought to exist everywhere.

---

61 The Bible Project: The Sabbath. https://www.youtube.com/watch?v=PFTLvkB3JLM

They had different motivations, background stories, and they always seemed to be at war or demanding something new from the humans who worshipped them.

But this God, the one later revealed as Yahweh, is a God who works and rests with boundless delight, doing everything necessary to bring flourishing to the creation underneath His loving rule and protection. After creating humanity on the sixth day, He invites them to rest with Him in fullness and joy.

He is no taskmaster god—no weak deity who needs something from humans to stay on the throne. Rather, in eternal bliss and unassailable self-sufficiency, He pauses from His work.

He rests in joy.

He delights in what He has made.

Chief among those delights are the apex of His creation—image bearers who bear His likeness and hold His breath inside them. So He calls them to rest in joy alongside Him.

SLAVERY OR SONSHIP

As we know by now, those created to be sons and daughters chose slavery instead. Slavery to the deceitful ideas of the serpent, ruinous lies, and the insatiable desires of animalistic flesh that was no longer filled and completed by the Spirit of God.

And then, in the course of Israel's history, God's people find themselves enslaved to Pharoah as well. God's miraculous and powerful rescue mission to free His people from the powerful tyrant of Egypt would become the Old Testament's primary metaphor for salvation. God heard their cries, and in grace did something to save them that they could have never done for themselves.

So Israel finds themselves back at Sinai, the very mountain where God revealed His name to Moses through fire, because He always keeps His promises. The voice booms again as all of Israel is within earshot this time, the mountain quakes, smoke rises.

Remember just how hard they had been working. They were forced to make bricks with no straw, mistreated by slave drivers, their lives made intentionally as difficult as possible to oppress them. The rulers of Egypt were "ruthless" in their demands (Exodus 1:13-14). The parallel account of the Ten Commandments in Deuteronomy 5 actually makes this connection to Egypt clear by adding: "Remember you were a slave in the land of Egypt" (Deut 5:15).

God sets Himself apart. He is a ruler, but a benevolent ruler. He is inviting His redeemed son Israel back into the rest and completeness of His intention. To take a whole day each week and live as if God is a Father who provides for His kids, and draws them into His own joyful rest.

You will not be slaves *anymore*, God is effectively saying. *You will now be sons, daughters.* Do not continue to act like you are in Egypt, because I've rescued you from that. Speaking of the delight found in this command, Peter Leithart writes:

> *"When idolatry and hypocrisy have been eliminated, when violence and infidelity and theft and lies have been chiseled off, this is what's left: a day of joy, and harmony among generations... This is the life God's son lives before his Father: Israel rejoicing with sons and daughters in the God who 'himself is festival.'"*
>
> **Peter Leithart, *The Ten Commandments***

What proof that He is for our good, that He would command a weekly celebration of rest, harmony, joy, and feasting? Sabbath is a clockwork reminder that we are not meant to be slaves to our work—but to rule over creation with our Father.

A COUNTERCULTURAL CALL

Our culture likely doesn't have a lot of emotional pushback to the idea of taking a Sabbath each week. We have plenty of practical pushback, as in, we aren't likely to actually *do* this, even if we understand all of the reasons why we should. But the *idea* sounds nice. Appealing, even. And we have some vague concept of it interwoven into a typical five day workweek.

But in the ancient world, the command for a weekly Sabbath was a novel idea. Life, on the whole, was less forgiving and convenient then. Crops had to be tilled, bread had to be kneaded, animals had to be tended—and there were only so many hours of daylight each week.

Could they really afford to take an entire day off from necessary life-sustaining activities?

Yes, God said. They could.

Because in doing so they would remember something even more important—that they have a Father who sustains their life. Who makes rain fall, and seed sprout, and breath exhale. So He calls them to come to His table, eat, relax, and laugh. To rest and settle into their createdness. A weekly reminder that they have a God who does what they can't do for themselves, who created them for more than anxious toil.

He was not concerned that the other nations did not function this way. That they had a practical advantage against Israel in success and progress due to an extra day. Rather, He said when the sojourner, or traveler, comes into your gates and stays on the Sabbath, they are to rest too. They would get a view into this new community God was creating, and would leave knowing there is something radically different about this nation.

There is something different about this *God.*

THE SANCTITY OF THE SABBATH

God has a different vision for life than any other king or society. He called His gathered ones to observe and keep this day as holy because He Himself is holy, and He blessed this day from the very beginning. As they observed this special day—gathered to worship Him and enjoy the fruits of the week's labor—the holiness of the day would seep into their souls. It would spark ancient memories, convictions that they were not meant for Egypt, but for an eternal country this day reminded them of.

So important was this call that it was not a mere suggestion for Israel. Yahweh would later implement strict punishment for Sabbath-breakers, testifying to the serious weight attached to obeying this commandment (Numbers 15:32-36).

A punishment of death may seem severe for breaking this commandment, but remember what God said about this day—it was *holy*. Just as He is holy. Which means it is untouchable, enshrined in glory, and aimed at communicating the untouchable nature of God Himself. Maybe the reason we find such trouble obeying the Sabbath is because we don't see much of anything as holy or untouchable in our culture. We have such little value for the moral foundation of sanctity that it's hard to fathom God responding in such a way, but again the problem is with us, not with Him. The holiness, or set-apartness, of this day would teach His image bearers about the holiness of God and the bountiful life He had for them.

The weekly Sabbath was also accompanied by yearly festivals, in addition to larger festivals that would happen every seven years or every forty-nine years. These were all meant to give joy and rest to God's people or even the land itself, and in some cases put an end to any debts people had incurred over time.

There is a restorative nature to everything built on the concept of Sabbath, and also a communal nature. It involved their kids and their livestock and servants and even sojourners. One person keeping the Sabbath is good for the whole group, so they were acting for each other's benefit as well. They were taking rest for themselves, but also giving rest—creating a humane culture where everyone could flourish.

As the Israelites learned in Egypt, we are not built for ceaseless work. Our bodies and souls break down when we reject our limits, our createdness. God, from Sinai, was calling His people back to the eternal rhythm set by Himself, to work and rest alongside the Father. To live under His gracious roof once more.

JESUS & THE SABBATH

With the historical context and creation purposes of Sabbath understood, it will come as no surprise that when Jesus began His earthly ministry in His hometown of Nazareth, He began on the Sabbath.

> And he came to Nazareth, where he had been brought up. And as was his custom, he went to the synagogue on the Sabbath day, and he stood up to read. 17 And the scroll of the prophet Isaiah was given to him. He unrolled the scroll and found the place where it was written,
>
> 18 "The Spirit of the Lord is upon me, because he has anointed me to proclaim good news to the poor. He has sent me to proclaim liberty to the captives and recovering of sight to the blind, to set at liberty those who are oppressed, 19 to proclaim the year of the Lord's favor."

₂₀ And he rolled up the scroll and gave it back to the attendant and sat down. And the eyes of all in the synagogue were fixed on him. ₂₁ And he began to say to them, "Today this Scripture has been fulfilled in your hearing."

Luke 4:16-21

He walks into His hometown synagogue, on the Sabbath day, and opens up the scroll to an ancient prophecy from Isaiah 61, which tells of the time when God will put everything to rights. When the ancient completeness and wholeness that was lost in the rebellion would be reinstated. He ends with the ultimate mic drop moment, declaring that He is the fulfillment of the promises He just read.

The implications of this are many, but just to name a few on the topic at hand:

1. **Jesus is our Sabbath rest.** There is no ambiguity in Jesus' claim when studied through the lens of Jewish history: He is saying He is the Messiah. He is the one who would fix everything broken by our sin. He would do so through a perfect life, sacrificial death, and supernatural resurrection. As the writer of Hebrews would later show, His perfection is what purchases Sabbath rest for us (Hebrews 4). We can now rest from our strivings to earn God's approval, because it's been imputed to us by grace.

2. **Jesus brings us to the ultimate Sabbath, the new creation.** His lifeless body lay motionless in the tomb during the Sabbath, and on the first day of a new week He rose, the firstfruits of a new world. Jesus ushers us into the coming kingdom of radiant light, where the old things have passed away and the new has come (Rev 21-22).[62]

3. **Jesus invites us to receive the Sabbath as a gift.** For Israel, observing the Sabbath was obviously mandatory, as it served as a sign of the covenant they had with Yahweh. Many Christian scholars argue that observance is no longer a commandment for Christians, because it has been fulfilled through Christ and no longer functions as a covenant sign.[63]

---

62 The Bible Project: The Sabbath. https://www.youtube.com/watch?v=PFTLvkB3JLM
63 For more see: "Is the Sabbath Still Required for Christians?" https://www.thegospelcoalition.org/blogs/justin-taylor/schreiner-qa-is-the-sabbath-still-required-for-christians/

Jesus taught that He is Lord, even over the Sabbath, and that the Sabbath was made for man, not the man for the Sabbath (Mark 2:27-28). Even if no longer a commandment for New Testament Christians, Jesus affirms that the rest and enjoyment of God and creation is for our good, and a gift to be received in gratitude.

To the debates about whether, or specifically how, Christians should observe the fourth commandment we would point back to the eternal wisdom of God. The character and nature of God resting in the beginning implies at the very least a "get to."

And it begs a simple question for modern people who love Jesus and need copious wisdom for life:

Do you want to be God's son? Do you want to be God's daughter?

Do you want to enter into the delight of doing nothing except enjoying the presence of your Father, and all the gifts He has provided?

COME TO ME, ALL WHO ARE WEARY

Jesus, again, is our model for sonship. In Matthew 11, He teaches that knowing the Father comes only through the Son, and that knowing the Father lifts heavy burdens:

> *At that time Jesus declared, "I thank you, Father, Lord of heaven and earth, that you have hidden these things from the wise and understanding and revealed them to little children; 26 yes, Father, for such was your gracious will. 27 All things have been handed over to me by my Father, and no one knows the Son except the Father, and no one knows the Father except the Son and anyone to whom the Son chooses to reveal him. 28 Come to me, all who labor and are heavy laden, and I will give you rest. 29 Take my yoke upon you, and learn from me, for I am gentle and lowly in heart, and you will find rest for your souls. 30 For my yoke is easy, and my burden is light."*
>
> **Matthew 11:25-30**

Jesus invites us into a life of Sabbath through Him. An existence devoid of anxious toil and striving, defined by rest and lightened burdens. He actually believes that following Him can take bone-weary, heavy-laden people and turn them into a non-anxious presence full of God's power and delight. This is a permanent invitation—not bound to a certain day of the week—and is overwhelming evidence that God is for our good.

It sounds almost too good to be true, and few of us would express that we regularly feel the way Jesus described. But what if a major reason our lived experience doesn't match what Jesus describes is because we haven't actually done what He called us to do?

What if we don't feel like a son because we don't act like the Son did?

Because we have not entered into and mimicked His practices, His way of life, His yoke...because we don't make it a habit to weekly enter into the delightful rest of God?

If you are weary from the slavish rhythm of your life that feels like one wave after another pounding you into oblivion—know that you are not the first to feel enslaved. There was a people whom God loved long ago who felt the same way, and God heard their cries. He rescued them from the ruthless demands surrounding them and brought them into a far better way of life, crafted by the eternal rhythm of God Himself.

The mountain boomed with undeniable wisdom and a beautiful opportunity. But obeying the command?

That was up to them.

INTERLUDE 7
ZOOMING IN: FOUNDATIONS LEFT & RIGHT

WE'RE ALL LIBERALS (TO A DEGREE)

If you take a group of Americans and compare us, say, to a group of medieval vikings, or to any other culture far removed from us—we would appear quite unified. In the span of history and the globe, there are big brush strokes that paint an insightful picture of our culture as a whole.

We are Americans, living in a democracy crafted by the trickled down ideas of the Enlightenment, a melting pot of people that share a backbone of ideology. We come from a long political history seeking to liberate the individual from oppression and tyrants. That is what this book has primarily focused on so far, the big picture.

But once you zoom down into our culture, you notice that there are significant differences among us, with political differences rising toward the top. One camp, the classical liberals (known as Republicans)—feels very far removed from progressive liberals (known as Democrats).

> *Disclaimer*: we have long taught that Jesus would not land perfectly in either camp today, and our pastors have varying degrees of disagreement on some political issues. We invite you to check your political elephants (or donkeys) at the door and look with insight into why others think differently than you. Also, some of the comments here are meant to be generalized and do not accurately reflect individuals on different points of the political spectrum.

A HISTORY OF LEFT & RIGHT

Interestingly enough, the directions that mark our political differences were not pulled out of thin air, but out of history in a literal room. In 1789, during the French Revolution that followed after our revolution, the French National Assembly was gathered. Massive upheaval of their government was on the table, and in the room supporters of tradition and the king gathered on the right side of the room, while supporters of the revolution gathered on the left side of the room.[64]

Baron de Gauville, a deputy in the Assembly, noted the historic moment:

"We began to recognize each other: those who were loyal to religion and the king took up positions to the right of the chair so as to avoid the shouts, oaths, and indecencies that enjoyed free rein in the opposing camp"

We know who won that debate, and the use of right-left language trickled down into many countries and governments, including ours. To this day in France, the left is called "the party of movement" and the right is called "the party of order."[65]

Sound familiar? To this day, the echoes of history can be traced in the two major political parties we have. Progressives want to progress in a certain direction, conservatives often hold up the caution flag, having more value for tradition as "the democracy of the dead."[66] Progressives think conservatives are stodgy and antiquated, conservatives think progressives are reckless and unwise.

We're still having the debate they were having in France in 1789, just in new and differing forms.

DIFFERENT PARTIES, DIFFERENT CATEGORIES

When using the 5 moral foundations from *The Righteous Mind* to zoom down into our particular culture, the implications are just as insightful and helpful as they are on a big-picture scale.

---

64 Left-Right Political Spectrum https://en.wikipedia.org/wiki/Left%E2%80%93right_politi-cal_spectrum
65 Ibid.
66 From G.K. Chesterton: "Tradition means giving votes to the most obscure of all classes, our ancestors. It is the democracy of the dead. Tradition refuses to submit to the small and arrogant oligarchy of those who merely happen to be walking about."

Just for fun, would you like to look again at the 5 foundations and take a guess on which ones would be prioritized most by progressives, and which ones would be prioritized most by conservatives? Then we will show the actual results of widespread research.

1. Care/Harm

2. Fairness

3. Loyalty

4. Authority

5. Sanctity

What would be your guess on which foundations are prioritized by each party?

Here are the results:[67]

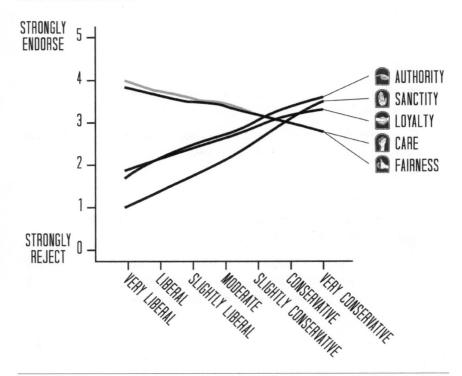

---

67 Scores are from the Moral Foundation Questionnaire, from 132,000 subjects, in 2011. The data is from YourMorals.org.

DECODING THE RESULTS

Here's what this graph shows:

- The further to the left a person reports to be, they tend to focus very heavily on the first two categories: care & fairness. Their marks for loyalty, authority, and sanctity are significantly lower.

- The further to the right a person reports being, they tend to prioritize the last 3 foundations: authority, loyalty, and sanctity.

- The concern for care/harm and fairness goes down as you move further to the right, but the grouping on the right side is still significantly closer than on the left.

- This research was compiled based on thorough questionnaires that can be taken at YourMorals.org. But hilariously enough, they found that even asking a question about what kind of dog you would prefer to own can fairly accurately predict your political leaning.

Here are the options participants were given:

1. The breed is extremely gentle. (Care/Harm)

2. The breed is very independent-minded and relates to its owner as a friend and equal. (Fairness)

3. The breed is extremely loyal to its home and family and it doesn't warm up quickly to strangers. (Loyalty)

4. The breed is very obedient and is easily trained to take orders. (Authority)

5. The breed is very clean and, like a cat, takes great care with its personal hygiene. (Sanctity)

It turned out that the majority of liberals picked 1 or 2, and the majority of conservatives picked 3 or 4. 5 was an anomaly—evidently everyone likes clean dogs. (*Sidenote*: this is a very fun exercise to do with friends.)

We'll press beyond the fascinating dog test in order to give a bit more on differences in each foundation.

CARE/HARM

Again, speaking broadly as a society we are all liberals in the proper sense, and greatly prioritize this foundation over many other cultures. But zoomed in on our culture, progressives prioritize it (along with fairness) more than conservatives. The prevention of harm, exclusion, or intolerance becomes a guiding principle.

There is much good in this, as liberals have been on the leading edge of caring for disadvantaged groups in our society. There is a reason why so many black Christians trend democratic, as the left has generally had a heightened concern for racial injustice. The plight of minorities or underrepresented voices such as the poor, women, immigrants, and children are pressing concerns for the left, and this can extend to the care of animals and the care of the Earth as well.

Conservatives, as Haidt points out, also prioritize care but sometimes let competing moral concerns outweigh this value. For example, conservatives tend to have more categories for the necessity of war even though some may get killed, they may argue more strongly for the death penalty in certain crimes even though it ends a life, and they may have more room for appropriate physical discipline of rebellious children. For conservatives more so than progressives, sometimes a degree of "hurt" is morally necessary and does not equate to a harm that must be rejected.

Haidt also notes that conservative caring is different, and that many times issues of care are directed towards those who have sacrificed for the group, such as soldiers. He gives a sharp example that "Save Darfur" is a great example of care from a liberal perspective, while "The Wounded Warrior Project" is a great example of conservative caring.[68]

FAIRNESS

Fairness is also greatly heightened in the scores of those reporting the most leftward leaning stance. It pairs well with the care/harm foundation, and is concerned about all being treated justly. This foundation points to the glaring hypocrisy of our founding documents as a nation that promised "liberty and justice for all" but went on to be built on the backs of slaves. Concerns about equality and social justice arise here, pointing to legitimate ways history affects the present.

---

68 Jonathan Haidt, *The Righteous Mind*, p.157.

This also bleeds heavily into economic concerns, with the left favoring redistribution of wealth and higher taxation far more than the right, and sometimes financial reparations for past societal harms done that were never given to provide historically oppressed citizens with a more equal footing. The left argues that the poor often have the deck stacked against them, and that hard work sometimes isn't enough to pull out of those widespread disadvantages.

Conservatives score lower on this foundation than progressives do without question, but Haidt makes an important distinction. He argues that conclusion is nuanced because conservatives actually define and think about the term *fairness* differently than progressives do.

For progressives, fairness implies equality, ideally in the form of equal *outcomes*. So the question is, "Does everyone end up in the same place?"

For conservatives, fairness means *proportionality*. The question is, "Does everyone have the same opportunity and access?"

In the conservative mind, equal outcomes are an impossibility, because the inputs of how hard people will work and what they will contribute will never be equal. They accept a degree of inequality as a natural part of life, and that to a large extent people will reap what they sow. Their triggers for fairness are often tripped in an opposite way, claiming it is unfair to take more from people who have worked the hardest to be successful and give it to those who have not worked as hard.

LOYALTY

This foundation is primarily about how much you identify with and remain loyal to the groups you find yourself to be a part of, and how loyalty to them is prioritized over concerns for out-groups. The best modern analogy for this foundation is likely the loyalty we feel for sports teams. When you cheer for your team and smirk at your rival, the loyalty foundation is activated.

Haidt argues from an evolutionary perspective that humans are tribalists by nature. We are "groupish," meaning we naturally group up for survival and flourishing. In the ancient world, having a large family or nation was tantamount for safety, because it gave you more humans to belong to and fight threats with.

The modern existence we share is quite different, and we don't feel much need at all to band together to fight off warring groups that might attack at any time. The nation and government we've created provides us with a historically unusual sense of safety from outside attacks. Especially if you grew up in a post-Cold War world, when have you ever felt genuinely threatened by another country? We can operate with uncommon swag that is not even fully known to us: *who is going to mess with us?*

Conservatives score higher on this foundation, and tend to have more national pride and unwavering appreciation and support for our military. Progressives tend to lean toward universalism and away from nationalism, seeing themselves as citizens of the world more than citizens of the United States. Haidt, who at that time proudly identified as a liberal, tells an interesting story about how he reacted after the attacks of 9/11. He said he found an inexplicable urge in himself to show national solidarity and pride by putting an American flag bumper sticker on his car, but being a professor he was slightly embarrassed of what his colleagues would think. So what was his solution? He put an American flag sticker on one side of his car, and a United Nations sticker on the other.[69]

This explains the controversy over NFL football players kneeling during the national anthem over the past several years. Many saw that as an incredibly reasonable and respectful protest, drawing attention to racial disparities and injustices that still occur in our country—primarily cases of police brutality towards African Americans. At the time, others saw those protests as an act of disloyalty to our nation and those who have died to protect the freedom we enjoy.

AUTHORITY

We are a nation of revolutionaries who threw off authority we didn't like, with historical roots going all the way back to political ideas birthed in the Enlightenment. The idea of having a King or Queen, as is the case in our ally Great Britain, is unthinkable to us. So again, we share far more common ground here than we sometimes think in the big picture.

We all descend from an anti-authority bias, from the founding of our country to the popular 1960s mantra, "Question authority." In another country that has a higher overall value for authority such as China, if there is an issue between a superior and a subordinate, the default view is that

---

69　Ibid, p.219

the subordinate is wrong. In America, it is often the opposite—we are far more likely than others cultures to believe that the superior is wrong.

But political differences arise here, with conservatives having more value and appreciation for authority as legitimate and necessary for human flourishing. The right tends to prioritize the need for children to respect and obey their parents, for citizens to obey the law and comply with law enforcement officers, for employees to submit to their superiors. They tend to see authority as a necessary component of fending off chaos and disorder, and therefore think of it more positively. (With some notable exceptions if it is felt that a government is infringing on certain rights.)

Progressives in general think about authority more negatively and suspiciously. They tend to believe any hierarchy is likely exploitative in nature and possibly even evil or unjust. In a debate where two parties are involved in a hierarchical relationship, they gravitate toward the side of the one under authority, and possibly question whether the hierarchy should exist at all because they can be misused and harm people.

SANCTITY

The last foundation tends to be easier to spot political differences in, simply because one side has tended to use it and another generally has not. Conservatives over recent decades have argued for the sanctity of marriage between a man and a woman, and the sanctity of life. Those on the far right of the spectrum have sanctity near the top of their concerns, while for those at the far left sanctity comes in last place.

This foundation argues that some things are wrong simply because they violate the sacred. Even if the thing in question doesn't directly harm anyone or if the victim one could point to is argued to not feel any pain. There is a different vision of flourishing here with at least functional categories for the divine, the sacred, and the profane. This does not mean conservatives have a robust biblical view of sanctity, or that they apply it consistently or only in honorable ways—just that the category and value are more likely to exist.

Progressives on the far left have little room for this foundation, arguing for human freedom in social issues to be prioritized. They also have little room for the shame that is attached to them, and advocate for a world where personal choices and consensual acts between adults are free of the weight of religious or cultural shame.

However, the foundation may surface in surprising ways on the left, as Haidt argues, in environmental concerns about the Earth's purity or impurity avoidance in the human body. Organic foods and high-end grocery stores can be avenues where this ancient concern rises up, as we seek to free the environment and our bodies from toxins or pollutants.

HOLD FAST TO WHAT IS GOOD

As Christians, we are swept up into this story and debate that is hundreds of years older than we are, happening all around us in ways we don't even see. Two different worldviews call to us constantly, preach their visions of the good life to us, and seek to make us their disciples.

Conservatives yell for us to abhor all things in the progressive worldview and cling to their vision of societal and economic flourishing. Which has many strong points, but also some problems.

Progressives scream for us to abhor the conservative worldview and cling to their vision of unrestricted freedom and economic equality. Which has some things that line up nicely with God's Kingdom, and others that are far from it.

Scripture says something altogether different: "Abhor what is evil; hold fast to what is good" (Romans 12:9). There is good and evil on both sides, and we are not called to be swept up totally into either vision, but stand with prophetic distance in our political engagement and call evil what is evil, wherever it is found.

We are called to be Christians first before we are Democrats or Republicans—our identity in Christ a far deeper anchor than any political party. Lord willing as we pursue that aim, we can use these categories to help understand the political, and therefore moral, differences that our neighbors have. In an environment that feels more polarized by the day, the wisdom found in these moral foundations can be helpful in calming the storm and getting to more beneficial conversations.

The insight here can help people start to understand each other rather than scream at one another. And Lord willing, help us build a foundation to share about the God who has a more beautiful vision of human flourishing than either of our political parties do.

CHAPTER 8

HONOR YOUR FATHER & MOTHER

AUTHORITY

Honor your father and your mother, that your days may be long in the land that the Lord your God is giving you.

Exodus 20:12

FOUNDATIONS COMING TO LIGHT: AUTHORITY

"Honor your father and mother' is the foundation upon which love for our neighbor is built."

Kevin DeYoung, *The Ten Commandments*

On first glance, this command may seem like a nice enough idea. Honoring your father and mother, whatever that means, doesn't sound so bad. We have Father's Day, Mother's Day. We buy cards and make phone calls. Does that count? If so, can we check this one off the list and move on?

To do so would be unwise, because this command is one where the more you study exactly what it means, the more you realize you may actually disagree with the Bible.

WHEN BIBLICAL VISION & CULTURE COLLIDE

We've been claiming through the entire book that our culture of secularism has less value for authority than hardly any other culture that has walked the Earth. Simply by being products of successful revolutions and setting up our *own* government our *own* way, our nation as a whole is a very unique historical minority. Over the past few hundred years, our country has been able to *create* what we want authority to look like—what it can and can't do, and how it works.

But still, saying we are a "question authority" culture may not have much impact if it's all you've ever known. What is water to a fish, after all?

In *The Righteous Mind*, Haidt tells a story describing the authority foundation that helps bring clarity. He was once riding in a taxi conversing with the driver who happened to be from the country of Jordan. After finding out that the driver had just become a father, he responded by asking what their family's plans were, and if they would remain in the U.S. to raise their son. The taxi driver said no, and his reasoning was unforgettable. He said:

"We will return to Jordan because I never want to hear my son say 'f*** you' to me."[70]

It was a jarring remark, because it's one that helps you see your culture. Here was a citizen of Jordan saying that if he stayed here to raise his child, he felt it to be a likely or inevitable outcome that his child would grow up to become the kind of person who would say such a thing to his or her parents.

That's not to say Jordan is the ideal culture either, but let the contrast sink in. It is a valuable indicator to help us notice the cultural waters we swim in that are so hard to see. Haidt finishes the thought with an important clarifier: "Now, most American children will never say such an awful thing to their parents, but some will, and many more will say it indirectly." How many more will think it?

If you think back to the Western Secular Liberalism video from Interlude 2, some important connections fall into place. The chart below shows some important shifts that took place during the Enlightenment and the birth of revolutions and Western civilization that profoundly affect the ways we think about raising children.

	Pre-Enlightenment	**Post-Enlightenment**
View of Human Nature	Inherently broken, in need of restraint.	Inherently good, need to be freed from restraint.
View of Authority	Inherently good and necessary, can become bad.	Inherently bad, can be used for good.
Pathway to Flourish	Accept limits and restraints.	Throw off limits and restraints.

---

70 *The Righteous Mind*, p.165

Pre-Enlightenment views had more in common with a Christian understanding of human nature, authority, and flourishing. The Bible says we are born in the image of God but also profoundly broken by sin, and in need of a new nature.[71] God's law and call to repentance through Christ sets up the limits and restraints we need to live as we were designed to, but it requires throwing off the fleshly desires we were born with.

Post-Enlightenment views were the opposite. Kids are born good, or at the very least blank slates (tabula rasa). The restraints and evil in their environment is what makes them turn out to be evil, so those need to be thrown off, so a human can be his or her true inner self. The historic view of freedom as being "freedom from" your base desires shifted into the modern view of "freedom to" chase all your desires.

Authority is highly suspect in the worldview of post-Enlightenment secularism, because it is thought to keep the pristine "inner child" from becoming the truest version of themselves.

There are significant areas of strength that our default worldview of secularism brings to how we approach parenting. We generally place a high value on children and approach them with a lot of warmth, care, and nurture, which is obviously fitting for any being made in the image of God—especially the smallest and most vulnerable. We marvel at the wonder of little ones, celebrate their achievements, want what is best for them, and will go to great lengths trying to get what we think is best for them. All of which is good and right.

But again, this book is not about the strengths of our culture, it's about the potential blindspots. And deep below all of the good lies some worldview issues that can be very difficult to see—one of which is illustrated by the story of the taxi driver. It begs the question: what happens to kids raised in a culture with so little value for authority? What are the spiritual outcomes of being trained to question authority at every turn?

How will children learn to honor God in a place such as this, raised by historically rare, anti-authority parents?

WHAT DOES HONOR MEAN?

The Hebrew word for "honor" is the word *kabod*, the same word used for "glory" or "weight." It is no small thing, and is not suggestive of occasional

---

71 Romans 3:9-26, Roman 6:1-14

half-hearted adherence to their instruction in your youth, or nice gestures of short appreciation when you grow old. Rather, it points in the same direction as the heart of honor we are to have towards God.

The logic for this is simple: our parents created us in their image like God created us all in His. He creates through fatherhood and motherhood, and sustains vulnerable life through parental care and protection. In many ways, parents are stand-ins for God. We learn to honor, respect, and obey God by first doing so with our parents.

The family was designed to be where we learn that authority is for our good, and that we often need to do things we don't want to, even when we don't understand why. Our parents are meant to teach us that we are not God—that getting everything we want would make us horrible people and destroy the community we inhabit. Civilizations and cultures are only able to flourish through the socialization that happens through families to foster social order, trust, and mutual respect.

Simply put, we learn how to behave in the world by learning how to behave in our family.

> *Disclaimer:* Obviously no parents are perfect. Many fall in the acceptable range, parenting and disciplining "as it seemed best to them" as Hebrews 12:10 states. But some are grossly harmful or abusive, and others train their children in sinfulness rather than training in righteousness. In the content that follows, there are obvious nuances to be drawn in how one would obey this commandment in that type of family.

Reformer John Calvin insisted that biblically, honor requires three things: "reverence, obedience, and gratitude."[72]

Reverence: Reverence means our heart posture toward our parents is the same as it is toward God. They are to be revered as holy to us—set apart, unequivocally higher than us. We are to have a default posture that "They are probably right and I am probably wrong, because they are smarter than me."

---

72 Kevin DeYoung, *The Ten Commandments.*

This does not tear down the affectionate familiarity much beloved in a parent/child relationship, but does mean there is a clear understanding of who holds the position of authority and who defers respectfully. Honor means giving an appropriate weight to the person and the position of parent, similarly to how the Israelites assigned weight to Yahweh as the mountain trembled. Blatant disrespect is not an option.

How you apply this may depend on the maturity of your parents and adapt as you grow older, but the default stance should be one of respect. Even when the role of father or mother is filled by an immature person, the position still commands reverence.

Obedience: Obedience means what we think it means, but probably with a significant qualifier to understand the weight of the word *kabod*. One way to describe the heart of a child formed with a biblical vision is found in the goal of "first-time obedience with a happy heart."[73] (Yes, we know that sounds fictitiously unattainable, but that's the vision of a flourishing heart under God's rule.)

When you stop and think about it, it may make more sense. When and how does God want you to obey Him? Does He count to ten from heaven? Is His goal for you to listen to Him on the seventeenth time He tells you not to do something? No, the goal is that His voice resonates with *kabod*, with glory and weight, where your heart trusts Him immediately and fully. Because doing so will be much better for you and others around you. We obey joyfully when we understand that He is for our good always.

Psychologist Jordan Peterson says you can tell the difference between kids who have learned to obey and kids who haven't. Kids who haven't tend to be conniving and brooding, generally disliked by other kids and adults. This sets them up miserably in life. These kids are doomed for a future of people not wanting to be their friends or bosses who don't want to employ them. Their lack of adequate socialization through their family will have adverse effects on the rest of their life (not to mention the lives of others), and they will wail at the unfairness of life, not realizing their problem's true cause.

Kids who have learned to trust authority and obey, however, become, in Peterson's words, "golden."[74] They glow with an attractive demeanor, having

---

73 This language came from Grace Church in Greenville, SC

74 Jordan Peterson, *12 Rules for Life*

learned humility and healthy interaction with authority, and therefore are welcome at any table or circle of friendship because other peers and adults want to be around them. They are set up for a far better life, with prospects galore and bosses that would love to hire and promote them.

Peterson makes a broad generalization and isn't speaking from a Christian perspective. But his logic is in line with God's command and is hard to deny. It's easy to see that God wants this outcome for us—for us to be golden— radiant with His love and wisdom that we have learned to gladly submit to.

And again, there are obvious differences between how a child applies this at three verses at thirty. The goal of obedience is that a child will learn to obey healthy authority while residing in the parent's home so that they'll be a certain kind of adult once they leave.

Gratitude: Building on reverence and obedience, gratitude makes note of the tremendous amounts of resources, time, energy, blood, sweat, and tears that go into parenting. As any parent of a toddler would realize, if kids only knew how much we do to protect them from harm and sustain their life, they might throw a few less tantrums and say a few more "thank yous." This awareness is able to grow as a child matures, and maybe finally sets in if you have children of your own and realize exactly what your parents did for you. Almost everyone thinks they would make an amazing parent right up until the moment they have kids.

While different seasons of our lives shape how we obey this command, the biblical vision is for the honoring of our parents to be a lifelong pursuit. We honor them in old age by heeding their wisdom, caring for them as needed, and giving them the glory and weight their position and effort deserves.

TEMPTATIONS TO (DIS)HONOR

When faced with this robust vision of what the Hebrew word for *honor* actually implies, it becomes easier to see that we have trouble with this. This is a difficult call for us who reside in our particular time and place in history.

Instead of having a weighty reverence, obedience, and gratitude for our parents, our culture can train us to do the opposite.

Instead of reverence for our parents, we diminish them. It is widely accepted for kids to talk back to their parents, roll their eyes, and disrespect them. That is viewed as normal, accepted, and potentially unavoidable in our culture—some parents see it as humorous, others frame it as the kid showing "executive leadership skills." Not so in the biblical vision. There, that disrespect is anything but normal, because treating God in those ways is also not celebrated or affirmed.

In ancient cultures and many around the world today, a person's value and esteem grows as they get older. Old age is a crown worn proudly that others admire and aspire to. Western cultures are "youth cultures," in that we prioritize and lift up the young, and relegate the old to the sidelines. God is not honored in this.

Instead of obeying our parents, we rebel against authority. In the biblical vision, obedience brings peace and order, while disobedience brings chaos and danger. It takes you outside of the boundaries where safety for yourself and others is found. The Scriptural view is that an undisciplined child grows up to be a dangerous adult, because kids who don't respect "no" turn into adults that don't respect the boundaries of others. A toddler who disrespects the "no" of his parents may be humorous, cute, annoying, or frustrating. But a grown man who disrespects the "no" of women in his life is a dangerous predator.

The Bible says, "Whoever spares the rod hates their children, but the one who loves their children is careful to discipline them" (Proverbs 13:24). Our culture, whether directly or indirectly, often says the opposite. Prevailing thought has become that parents who make their children obey are too authoritative, that discipline is harsh, and that restrictions of freedom may inhibit their individuality.

Instead of appropriate training to form our kids into people who don't need supervision to act well, we overfunction and manage their disobedience. Kids see these opportunities early, and seek to rule and dominate whatever they can. Our culture is full of six-year-olds who run households in a state of Kindergarchy[75]. They think it's good for them, their parents think it's healthy—but in reality, it's crushing their to their long-term development. Because six-year-olds are meant to obey authority, not give orders.

---

75 It appears the first use of this term may have been in a 2008 essay by Joseph Epstein: The Kindergarchy https://www.ipce.info/library/newspaper-article/kindergarchy-every-child-dauphin

This tendency toward willfulness and lack of respect for authority of course does not stay focused only on parents, but blossoms outward into all areas of life.

Instead of being grateful for our parents, we dissect them. Like we said earlier, there are people who had truly devastating parents, and those wounds are real and must be acknowledged and dealt with. There are some in our churches who could try valiantly to find things to be grateful for about a parent, and struggle with the charge due to immense sin issues or abandonment.

But there are tons of parents who fall into the category of *not perfect—but overall pretty good. Fairly healthy. Definitely not a monster.*

And our culture does not breed gratitude for them in the same amounts that it breeds blame. When encouraged to look deeply into your story, you will find plenty of wounds from your family of origin. Those can be worked through while still seeking to honor your parents, but that process can also turn into a dissection so thorough that it would slice through all of us.

From the Bible's perspective we are sinners who also have been wounded— not wounded people who also sin sometimes. So it is a problem if we spend more time and energy scrutinizing our parents to explain what's wrong with us than we do scrutinizing ourselves.

We are called to honor our parents, not eviscerate them. You can be honest about their failures and honor them at the same time, but it will take effort not to move toward ingratitude and arrogance. The worst part about such a spirit is that should you become a parent yourself, you are destined to become what you despise: an imperfect parent who wounds their kids.

THAT YOUR DAYS MAY BE LONG

Paul repeats this command in Ephesians 6, noting that this is the first command with a promise attached to it. The retelling of the commandments in Deuteronomy 5, which Paul quotes from, adds some context to the promise: *"that your days may be long, and that it may go well with you in the land that the Lord your God is giving you"* (Deuteronomy 5:16).

Scholars tend to agree that this was not a one-to-one law that if you obey your parents you will live a long and happy life. There are good and honorable children and adults who die untimely deaths, so this is not some foolproof formula. Rather, it is a general truth that when we learn to respect authority and live under God's design, things go well for us. So the command is not just about length of life, but quality of life as well. Positioning yourself under God's authority through the structures He sets in place leads to a fruitful and enjoyable life.

For the ancient Israelites living under God-given civil laws of a theocracy, there were practical concerns as well. In Deuteronomy 21, as Moses is giving the laws for how the nation of Israel was supposed to function, he gives a shocking example that shows just how serious God is about this command, and how concerned He is with the damage that will be caused to others and a society by breaking it in severe ways.

> *"If a man has a stubborn and rebellious son who will not obey the voice of his father or the voice of his mother, and, though they discipline him, will not listen to them, ₁₉ then his father and his mother shall take hold of him and bring him out to the elders of his city at the gate of the place where he lives, ₂₀ and they shall say to the elders of his city, 'This our son is stubborn and rebellious; he will not obey our voice; he is a glutton and a drunkard.' ₂₁ Then all the men of the city shall stone him to death with stones. So you shall purge the evil from your midst, and all Israel shall hear, and fear."*

> ### *Deuteronomy 21:18-21*

This is an eye-popping punishment for our culture. It is a civil law of ancient Israel, and certainly does not apply to us—we are under the covenant of grace and are not citizens of ancient Israel. It also shouldn't be confused with modern, mentally ill parents who have killed their children. In the Old Testament, only God had the right to dictate the acceptable circumstances to end a life.

But it does give a category for someone being so evil, so harmful for others and a society, that their continued presence is a threat. An undisciplined man is a danger, and they cause unspeakable harm to others through murder, rape, crime, violence, or addiction. And for Israel, God decided that such a man who refused all attempts to get him to accept authority was bad for the world.

As reformer and pastor John Calvin bluntly stated, *"Nature itself ought, in a way, to teach us this. Those who abusively or stubbornly violate parental authority are monsters, not men."*

TRADING PLACES WITH THE REBELLIOUS SON

The shock doesn't end with that ancient civil law. The very next verses provide a shadow of how God would act in unthinkable ways to rescue people like that rebellious son from wrath both worldly and divine. The following verses of Deuteronomy chapter 21 go on to state:

> *"And if a man has committed a crime punishable by death and he is put to death, and you hang him on a tree, 23 his body shall not remain all night on the tree, but you shall bury him the same day, for a hanged man is cursed by God. You shall not defile your land that the Lord your God is giving you for an inheritance."*

> ***Deuteronomy 21:22-23***

This is the warning that made Jesus' death by crucifixion so unimaginably embarrassing to the Jews that hoped He was the redeemer God promised. No Messiah, in their mind, would ever be put to death, and certainly not hanged on a tree—because that was cursed by God Himself. An act that defiles the very land it occurs on, polluting the Earth with its shame.

It was an act reserved for the worst of the worst. The people who are so bad for the world because they pollute society with their egregious crimes. The rebellious sons who refused to honor their father and mother, and turned into a reckless, dangerous human.

What they didn't understand was that on the cross, the Son of God was trading places with the rebellious son.

Jesus, who had only and always revered the voice of His Father, obeyed His will, and showed gratitude for His loving care—traded places with he who had done none of that. With those rightfully under God's wrath.

He obeyed to the uttermost to save those who refused to obey. He sweat blood in the Garden of Gethsemane while submitting to His Father's perfect will, and willingly walked into unimaginable beatings, torture, and humiliation. And when He cries out to His Father in agony while suffocating on the cross, we see the unimaginable truth:

The perfect Son took the place of the rebellious son, so the condemned son could go free.

This insight gives new weight to the famous story of the prodigal son, who was also a drunkard and a glutton.[76] (Which is the same language used to describe the rebellious son in Deuteronomy 21.)

Technically, under ancient Jewish civil law, the father in the story would have been justified not only rejecting this wayward son of his, but also could have had him stoned so his misdeeds could no longer harm the world. Instead of that, what does the father do?

He watches for the son. He sees him when he's still a long way off, gathers up his robe, and runs.

This running was culturally undignified for an old man. But his undignified act of love was about to re-dignify his shamed son. When he meets him, he embraces his son and his act of repentance—stopping his apology short to rejoice and celebrate his return.

> *"For this my son was dead, and is alive again; he was lost, and is found.' And they began to celebrate."*

Luke 15:24

What good news this is to us who have disrespected and dishonored both our parents and God in numerous ways. The hard truth is that on some level, we are all the rebellious son, the rebellious daughter, the prodigal. It is not some far off criminal who rightfully deserves the wrath of God, but you and I. The wages of our sin is death, as Romans 6:23 says.

But...isn't that a beautiful word?

But it also says the free gift of God is eternal life in God's family through Christ.

But we have a perfect Son who traded places with us, so we could go free.

But we have a Father who doesn't hold our grievous acts against us, who instead kicks up the dust behind Him as He runs to hug our necks.

We have had the earth-shattering gift of sonship, of daughtership, bestowed upon us. This gift causes angels to stop in their tracks and look in awe as God welcomes us to His very own table.

---

76 Kevin DeYoung, *The Ten Commandments*

So may we as sons and daughters enter God's family with the gratitude and respect our spiritual adoption deserves.

And for our earthly parents—the imperfect but meaningful stand-ins for God given to us by grace—may we learn to hold them high in honor, in every way possible.

INTERLUDE 8
THE GOSPEL OF SECULARISM

"It is a safe thing to trust Him to fulfill the desires He creates."

Amy Carmichael

The story of the world is that in the beginning, God declared Himself to be God, with sole control over what is good and what is evil. That was the key to Eden.

We said no thanks, and have suffered the effects ever since.

But we have not simply suffered the effects, we've tried to manage and heal the pain on our own, as humans are prone to do. To come up with solutions that will save us, get us back to the primordial promised land we feel in our hearts we were made for but cannot find in the world.

Theologians call these attempts at self-salvation "salvation schemas." They are rubrics of understanding, or stories, that appeal to our desire for what has gone wrong to be put right again. Each has a form of "gospel," or good news, that promises to fix what is broken, and generally they follow a simple formula that feels an awful lot like many stories you have heard:

The Structure of Salvation Schemas	
Setting	Introduces the characters, tells us a bit about the world they live in and what their purpose is in that world.
Conflict	A central tension is introduced, normally through the help of an antagonist.
Climax	A hero emerges and strikes the fatal blow to the antagonist. The power of the conflict is overcome, though there is still residual effect and collateral damage to be cleaned up.
Resolution	A utopian conclusion is reached. Everything is put back right. Order and hope are restored.

Of course, Christianity can be viewed through this lens as well, being the true story of reality itself.

	The Christian Salvation Schema
Setting	In Genesis 1-2, it becomes clear that God is the central character of reality. And He makes humanity in His image. Their world is good, fruitful and their purpose is to work creatively with God bringing more and more order and life to the wildness of creation.
Conflict	In Genesis 3, we meet our antagonist, Satan. The serpent comes to Adam and Eve and convinces them to reject God's authority and rebel against Him. This is the central conflict in human history. We have sinned and joined Satan in rejecting God.
Climax	Starting in Genesis 3, the Old Testament keeps pointing ahead to One who is to come. A Messiah who would come and crush the serpent. All of this is fulfilled in Jesus' perfect life, death and resurrection. Jesus defeats the serpent, conquers the power of sin and death, and saves us by grace.
Resolution	We live in the falling action of human history—the church age—where we are working to see Jesus' kingdom come. We are waiting for Jesus' return where He will institute His kingdom once and for all, as we see in Revelation 21 when the New Jerusalem comes down from heaven and meets Earth.

This is the story God grounds us in—the truest true story that has ever existed. This, God says, is the way back to Eden, or more specifically the improved Eden of the new heavens and the new Earth.

But there are still competing stories everywhere we look. Consider, as examples, a few different common cultural ways of trying to solve our deepest problems:

The Romance Salvation Schema	
Setting	We were all made for romantic love. Romantic connection in marriage or random hookups are the height of human fulfilment.
Conflict	Loneliness or unfulfillment. We're all alone until we find our soulmate we've been separated from! Anyone or anything that gets in the way of you finding your "one" is the antagonist.
Climax	Finding the one. In movies this often happens in the airport. Or the rain.
Resolution	"They lived happily ever after." You'll never be alone ever again. Life will be happy and complete. The most modern version of this is maybe you married the wrong one to begin with and that's why you're unhappy... but an affair with the actual right one...that'll solve it!

The Sports Fan Salvation Schema	
Setting	"Last year." Last year was tough. There were some wins. Some losses. But we, the faithful, are loyal, sacrificial fans who have been denied the glory due our team.
Conflict	Someone or something is in the way of our team achieving the glory we have always known they deserve. It can be an idiot coach, an idiot quarterback or an idiot team owner. Sometimes it's a series of unfortunate injuries. Sometimes it's one specific team or rival that's got our number. It's *always* the referees.
Climax	Winning the 'ship. The last second game winning 3 pointer... that will never be forgotten. The hail mary pass that is tipped 6 times and miraculously caught.
Resolution	"Next year." Basking in the glow of the victory. Taunting your rivals.

	The Political Salvation Schema
Setting	We are a country in need of some reform. If you're conservative—we need to get back to the glory days. If you're liberal—we need to move forward to the glory days.
Conflict	We're beset with certain cultural, environmental, economic and bureaucratic ills. We need a hero. We need a new candidate who will overcome all the bad ideas of the last party's winning candidate and usher our country into Utopia.
Climax	Your candidate wins.
Resolution	Enjoy the president's hopeful promises for a few months while the opposing party is already getting ready for their version of the political salvation schema coming 4-8 years from now.

With all those examples aside, we'll end with one last example that sums up some of the cultural insights we've been talking about throughout this book. The worldview of secularism also has a salvation schema, and it is deeply ingrained, pernicious, and hard to see.[77]

	The Secular Salvation Schema
Setting	The inner child. The inner self. At some point I had this happiness, this innocent, joyful self before I was spoiled and ruined by my environment and my family of origin. Some things you may hear that point to this might be:
	"I've had a terrible season at work and I just need to go camping because I need to find myself, connect with myself."
	"I feel like my inner child spoke for the first time in a long time."
	"I just don't know if my restrictive marriage/spouse sees the real me and will let me be my real self."

---

77 This chart and some of the language it includes was adapted from an episode of the podcast: This Cultural Moment: The Secular Salvation Schema https://podcasts.apple.com/us/podcast/this-cultural-moment/id1342868490?i=1000424642058

Conflict	Trauma that harmed my inner self, or restrictions that keep my inner self from being who it was supposed to be.
	Of course, trauma is real and many experience it. It should be brought to Jesus and community for healing. But in this worldview, remember, we are hunting for dragons, so the concept of trauma expands. Decades ago in earlier versions of the DSM (used by mental health professionals for diagnoses), the word "trauma" was reserved for events that would be traumatic for almost anyone (war, rape, torture, etc.).[78] It was not subjective, but objective.
	In popular culture this term, like others, has endured something called "concept creep" where it has crept downward and outward to encompass more categories and lesser degrees of difficulty. Increasingly the concept of trauma is defined *subjectively* by those who go through difficulty or pain and name it trauma.[79]
	Unsurprisingly, in this worldview restrictions on freedom are thought to actually cause trauma, because they keep the inner self from being true to itself.
	Sin in this worldview is low self-esteem and unhappiness. Anything that makes us feel bad about ourselves or feel shame is denounced. This can broaden where anything difficult is seen as sin—the hard conversation, the concept I don't want to think about. Even something as simple as going to work can feel evil because it's so restrictive.
	This correlates well with the avocado view of the self discussed previously—because we see ourselves as fragile. Whereas other cultures see humans as *anti-fragile*—like human muscles, that need stress and difficulty to grow and strengthen.[80]

78 *Coddling of the American Mind*, Johnathan Haidt & Greg Lukianoff
79 "Concept creep" and the ideological changes of words like "trauma" and "abuse" over time are considered at length in *Coddling of the American Mind*. When we use the most severe words to describe increasingly less severe experiences, it can cause emotional and mental chaos, and most importantly—cheapen the experience of those who have lived through severe adverse circumstances.
80 Author and professor Nassim Nicholas Taleb used the phrase antifragile in his book titled *Antifragile*. He differentiates between 3 types of things: 1) things that are fragile (like ceramic), 2) things that are resilient (like plastic cups), and 3) things that are antifragile (like human muscle or immune systems).

Climax	Rediscovering who you really are. Throwing off all restrictions to finally express who you believe yourself to be deep on the inside. This is the *Eat, Pray, Love* story: I'm gonna leave my job and go travel the world.
	This is a moral vision—connecting with your inner self is seen as holiness. Restrictions threaten your ability to be true to yourself, so the path to holiness in secularism is refraining from commitments or authority outside of yourself.
Resolution	Self-actualized happiness. All of human life and society will flourish when we are free to do whatever we want with no one telling us what to do at all.
	The end-game is a society of completely freed individuals, unencumbered by restrictions, replete with unassailable rights, and able to define good and evil for themselves through the creation of their "truth."

When you stop to think about it, it's everywhere, isn't it? It is so pervasive that it's hard to even see or pick up on. And it's not entirely bad—there are some redeemable things woven throughout. But taken as a whole, it is remarkably spiritually dangerous.

Because the "gospel" of secularism is no gospel at all. It leads us away from the home we were made for. Away from the true freedom found within benevolent boundaries to the unrestricted "freedom" where we are little gods and goddesses.

Away from Jerusalem, and toward Emmaus.

All of which may feel like it is for our good, but is resoundingly not. Because the New Jerusalem—the city our souls pine for—will not be found through rediscovering yourself. The empty calls of Emmaus offer cold comfort, and the howling peddlers of secularism will only lead to shallow and fleeting glories. There is no lasting good news to be found there—only the redundant miseries of never-ending self-focus.

But that shimmering city coming down out of the clouds? It calls our eyes *up, up, up*—to a Kingdom far bigger than ourselves. To a place where there is indeed a King we have to submit to, but He's the *best* King. To a place whose radiant glory is only found through the humility of the cross, accepting our createdness, our not-God-ness, and our need for salvation.

And in return, it offers nothing short of everlasting joy.

CHAPTER 9
YOU SHALL NOT MURDER

CARE/HARM SANCTITY

You shall not murder.

Exodus 20:13

"For thus said the Lord of hosts, after his glory sent me to the nations who plundered you, for he who touches you touches the apple of his eye..."

Zechariah 2:8

HE'S A HUMAN

On May 25th, 2020 George Floyd was killed while being arrested by four police officers in Minneapolis, Minnesota. According to eyewitness video and criminal complaints, officer Derek Chauvin kneeled on Floyd's neck for a total of 8 minutes and 46 seconds, including more than 2 minutes after he became unresponsive.

In the gruesome, heart wrenching video George Floyd is heard saying "I can't breathe!" and even pleads for his deceased mother, while bystanders yell that he is in distress and is no longer responsive. One bystander is heard saying "He's a human!"

At the time of this writing, officer Derek Chauvin has been convicted of second degree murder, and the other three officers have been charged with aiding and abetting second degree murder. The lengthy, videotaped killing sparked widespread national dialogue about police brutality and systemic racial injustice.

The painful reality in our country is that historically speaking, black life has not always mattered as much as it matters to God. That is something that should make us angry, because it makes God even more angry.

After peaceful protests of athletes kneeling during the national anthem sought to draw attention to the different experiences African Americans still have in this country, this video of murder-by-kneeling was a tragically painful bookend. In the aftermath of Floyd's death, the Minneapolis Police Cheif Medaria Arradondo rightfully denounced the blatant disregard for "the sanctity of life" he wanted to uphold in the department.[81]

The history of racial injustice added a heartbreaking dynamic to an already atrocious act, because what watchers saw was the unnecessary taking of a life that is inherently precious to God. And as Zechariah says, whoever messes with an image bearer messes with the apple of God's eye (Zechariah 2:8).

"NOT KILL" & *IMAGO DEI*

The sixth commandment is one we easily understand the importance of, since murder is the ultimate harm one can do to another. In Hebrew, the command consists of only two words: *not kill*, or *not murder*. No further reasoning is given, but ancient Israelites would have understood that it had previously been given in Genesis 9:[82]

> *Whoever sheds the blood of man,*
>   *by man shall his blood be shed,*
>   *for God made man in his own image.*

> **Genesis 9:6**

Humans are made in God's image and therefore have inestimable dignity and worth. The Latin phrase, and theological term for this is *imago dei*. Human life is sacred and holy, because we breathe the very breath of God. We bear His likeness, and that is no light concern.

God treats attacks on the *imago dei* of His creation with the utmost severity. He sees a violation of this command as an attack not only on an innocent victim, but an attack on Himself. It is a grave offense to take a life, to snuff out the created image of God. One worthy, in some circumstances, of your life being taken in response.

---

81 "'This is the right call': Officers involved in fatal Minneapolis incident fired, mayor says" https://kstp.com/minnesota-news/minneapolis-police-george-floyd-death-/5741256/
82 Peter Leithart, *The Ten Commandments.*

CATEGORIES & CLARITY

Scholars argue about whether the word should be translated in English as *murder* or *kill*, with some arguing that the term murder is too specific. The Hebrew word often means "murder," but the same verb describes what we call "manslaughter."[83] Translation issues aside, the weight of the commandment lands with an undeniable point: we are to regard human life as so precious and sacred that we dare not take a life intentionally in murder, and we are to take every precaution possible to avoid taking a life unintentionally. God created human life, so He alone dictates the circumstances where it should end: not us. To do so would be to take the role of God in our hands, and decide through intentionality or through negligence that another image bearer should die.

WHAT THE SIXTH COMMANDMENT SEEMINGLY ALLOWS

In the context of laws given around this commandment, we do see some categories of life-taking that were not forbidden by this commandment. Some examples include: killing in self-defense (Exodus 22:2-2), capital punishment (Genesis 9:6, Exodus 21:23-25), and necessary war.[84]

- **Killing in self-defense:** Exodus 22 gives helpful clarity meant to teach that if killing in self-defense was the only option to survive, it is not a violation of the sixth commandment. However, if it is found that killing was not necessary, it is a violation.

- **Capital punishment:** In the Old Testament, capital punishment for murder was not seen as a violation of this commandment, but a severe punishment meant to uphold the sacredness of human life and warn others not to take it.[85] The famous saying about this comes from Exodus 21: "an eye for an eye...a life for a life." In our modern times, there is still debate about whether capital punishment is ever the best choice and even in states that practice it, we reserve it for the most extreme violators and situations. Some are categorically against it, thinking of it as an unacceptable form of punishment.

---

83 Ibid.
84 Kevin DeYoung, *The Ten Commandments.* While these categories are supported by Old Testament passages, there is debate among Christian scholars about which are still viable under a New Testament Christian ethic.
85 God's statements in Genesis 9:6 were a foreshadowing of this law.

However, remember the context of the ancient world—which was populated by tribal, warring groups whose conflicts escalated quickly. This guideline would have been countercultural for its original audience:

"Gandhi once said, 'An eye for an eye makes the whole world blind,' and we think, 'Oh, that's right. That's not a very good law.' But within the context of the ancient Near East, this was quite a humane law. It said, 'An eye for an eye, a tooth for a tooth, and a wound for a wound,' instead of, 'Your head for an eye, your family for a tooth, and your tribe if you offend me.' It set the precedent that the punishment must fit (and not exceed) the crime. Life for life—no less and no more.

Kevin DeYoung, *The Ten Commandments*

- **Necessary war:** God obviously sent Israel into battle through the Old Testament, showing that He has a category for just war as a necessity in a world shattered by sinful humans. However, this does not mean all wars are just wars, and some Christian scholars argue with the continuation of this category altogether. At minimum Christians should thoughtfully ask questions about the justness of war in regards to our support of and willingness to fight in wars waged by a secular state.[86]

WHAT THE SIXTH COMMANDMENT PROHIBITS

The totality of two words, *not kill*, prohibits any form of life-taking outside of the rare occasions mentioned above. It obviously prohibits premeditated, intentional murder. The punishment for such an act was swift and severe, meant to keep it from happening again.

But again, it also prohibits life-ending acts that occur as a result of negligence or recklessness. In Exodus 21, an ancient example is given that has modern implications. It says if an ox gores someone to death and it hasn't been known to be violent before, the owner of the ox is not liable for the accidental death. But if the ox has been prone to gore previously, and the owner didn't take precautions to keep it away from others, the ox and the owner were to

---

86 The "just war theory" is contested by Christian scholars and some argue that the New Testament ends the acceptability of just war and advocates for some form of Christian pacifism. For introductory research on differing views see the book *War: Four Christian Views.*

be put to death.[87] Similar demands were made for building a fence around your roof, to keep others from falling off (Deuteronomy 22:8). These were commands to protect human life through diligence and wisdom.

A modern equivalent of this type of reckless life-taking might be driving while distracted by your phone, and killing another person (which would certainly include drunk driving as well). We are called to treat human life as so holy that we take the utmost care not to end it through careless behavior.

Even when the utmost precautions are taken, however, the Old Testament still acknowledges that truly accidental deaths sometimes happen. In the civil laws governing their nation, a family member or friend of someone who was murdered took on the role of "avenger of blood," and was lawfully allowed to kill the murderer (Numbers 35:21). But in cases of accidental death, God instituted cities of refuge that the person who accidentally killed could flee to for safety. There they would be kept from danger from pursuing avengers until they faced a trial. If the death was pronounced as a genuine accident, they were free from consequences and allowed to stay in the city of refuge (Numbers 35).

In an ancient world that was comparatively brutal compared to ours, this was a means of grace that kept one tragedy from becoming another and leading to a perpetual cycle of violence.

Moving toward more modern questions, the sixth commandment also prohibits suicide, euthanasia, and abortion.[88]

SUICIDE

The logic here is simple: your life is not yours to take. You are made in God's image, so your life is untouchably sacred. God alone decides when it will end. This is doubly true for a Christian whose life has been "bought with a price" (1 Corinthians 6:20).

Suicide is always tragic and often results from devastating mental illness and/or demonic oppression. And there is nowhere in Scripture that says it is an unforgivable sin. But it is most certainly a sin, and that is said with the utmost compassion. Self-murder is murder still, and compassion for mental illness aside—taking your own life is an egregiously selfish act that will cause unspeakable harm to those that love you for generations.

---

87 Exodus 21:28-29
88 Kevin DeYoung, *The Ten Commandments.*

It is simply not an option for Christians seeking to honor God with our breath. As Pulitzer Prize winning author Marilynne Robinson said in her novel *Gilead*, "There are a thousand thousand reasons to live this life, everyone of them sufficient."

EUTHANASIA

Because we live in a culture that so prioritizes issues of care/harm and personal autonomy, the topic of assisted suicide has gained traction in public thinking. If someone is hurting and doesn't want to continue living, is it compassionate for medical professionals to help them end their life? A prevailing ethic of autonomy above all else makes honoring their freedom to choose sound reasonable to some.

But if all of life is truly sacred and precious, then doing so would not be compassionate at all. The lives of the elderly, the chronically ill, the disabled, and the severely mentally ill are just as meaningful and precious as the healthy. We should do what we can to help them ease their pain, but agreeing to help them end their life when God has not done so is taking a position we were not designed to hold. We, as image bearers, do not decide when the life of another image bearer ends.

While continued existence for some can be painful for some and trigger our care foundations, causing us to ask difficult questions—we must remember a truth our culture constantly seeks to escape from: suffering is a part of life. Suffering is coming for us all, and part of what it teaches us is that we were made for another world.

In a way, the Covid-19 pandemic and the moral questions it brought shone light on this reality: the lives of the old and the sick are valuable, and worth guarding in any way possible.

ABORTION

Before we proceed, we recognize this section may be painful for some. There is abounding grace at the feet of Jesus. And while we need to have a considerable, clear discussion about how our culture thinks about abortion, we also recognize that most abortion-minded women are not "uber-political...calculating killers."[89] They are afraid, many times

---

89 "Most Abortion-Minded Women Aren't Calculating Killers. They're Afraid." https://www. thegospelcoalition.org/article/women-abortions-devious-murderers/

alone—abandoned by pathetic men unworthy of the responsibility sex brings. And sometimes aggressively pushed by angry husbands, boyfriends, or parents. As one writer put it:

> *Most women seeking abortions aren't uber-political. They aren't members of the aggressively pro-abortion, Twitter-argument-waging, shout-your-abortion crowd. They aren't calculating murderers. They're afraid.*
>
> *Abortion is a great evil. It's left an ugly, gaping hole in the world where millions of image-bearing children should be. While the church has largely excelled at calling this despicable spade a spade, she often fails to see this picture: a young, often impoverished, terrified woman—who knows her baby is a human!—but considers abortion anyway. Fear is incredibly potent.*
>
> **Maria Baer**

With those important disclaimers aside, Scripture has some deep critique of our culture's thought about abortion. The Bible is unequivocally clear about when life begins. David, reflecting in Psalm 139, states a beautiful truth about God's involvement in creating human life in the womb:

> *For you formed my inward parts;*
> *   you knitted me together in my mother's womb.*
> *14 I praise you, for I am fearfully and wonderfully made.*
> *Wonderful are your works;*
> *   my soul knows it very well.*
> *15 My frame was not hidden from you,*
> *when I was being made in secret,*
> *   intricately woven in the depths of the earth.*
> *16 Your eyes saw my unformed substance;*
> *in your book were written, every one of them,*
> *   the days that were formed for me,*
> *   when as yet there was none of them.*

Psalm 139:13-16

Human life begins at conception, once a female egg is fertilized with male sperm. As expectant parents have quickly learned at early ultrasounds, the sound of a beating heart occurs around 6 weeks gestation. At 9 weeks, the clear figure of a tiny human can be made out.

These are no "lumps of cells," as some would have you believe. They are not simply "potential humans." They are humans, made in the image of God, with beating hearts. Each of us reading this were exactly such as they. This is the means through which God creates human life, and it is worth marveling at.

Their frames are not hidden from God. Rather, they are seen, celebrated, and adored as the image bearers they are.

The ancient Greek Christian creed *The Didache* forbade the practice of abortion, and notably, the original version of The Hippocratic Oath— the oath most medical students take—did as well. There are difficult things to consider in cases of rape, incest, the viability of the child or true danger to the health of the mother. But according to available research, those complex, agonizing scenarios are not close to the primary motivations behind abortion.[90]

There is an impassioned, desperate attempt by some in our culture to make abortion simply a choice that carries no shame or moral weight. There is a concerted effort to rebrand it as "reproductive healthcare," as if it is simply equivalent to going in for a routine procedure. Activists have started Twitter hashtags for #shoutyourabortion, encouraging people to publicly tell their abortion stories and why they are glad they made the best decision for themselves.

Notice the reasoning given in one Twitter user's story:

> *"I had an abortion when I was young, and it was the best decision I have ever made. Both for me, and for the baby I didn't want, and wasn't ready for, emotionally, psychologically and financially.*

---

90 The most recent study of the reasons why women have abortions by The Guttmacher Institute, a pro-abortion group, was performed in 2004. In a study where multiple reasons could be chosen, rape and incest combined accounted for less than 1.5%. A physical problem with the mother's health accounted for 12%, and a possible problem effecting the health of the baby accounted for 13%. "Reasons US Women Have Abortions: Quantitative and Qualitative Perspectives" https://www.guttmacher.org/sites/default/files/pdfs/pubs/psrh/full/3711005.pdf

So many children will end up in foster homes. So many lives ruined. So very cruel."[91]

Did you catch the moral foundation used to justify the abortion? Not going through with ending the baby's life, in this woman's perspective, would have caused "harm" to the unwanted child. He or she may have ended up in foster care, or had their life "ruined." Keeping an unwanted baby would have been "so very cruel" to the child. (Note that this person used care/harm language to justify an act that demonstrably destroyed a human life. The logic literally says letting a human live would have caused more harm than good—without consulting the opinion of that human.)

It appears in all of this, and the many likes and retweets the tweet received, that there is no acknowledgement that a baby in a womb, with a beating heart—was either poisoned, destroyed by a suction pump, torn apart limb by limb in the womb, or possibly subjected to even more barbaric treatment (such as with partial birth abortions).

But no—keeping the child, trying to take care of it, and giving it a chance in life—*that's* what would have been cruel?

Because he or she may have grown up poor or gone into foster care?

Abortion has been normalized in our sin-racked world. It is largely hidden from view, and we can tend to forget about it. But the fact is, over 50 million babies have been aborted in our country since *Roe vs. Wade* was passed in 1973.[92]

50 million image bearers, at least.

50 million lives forcefully ended without their consent.

To put in perspective, 50 million is roughly the current population of California and Georgia combined.[93] Or, at the time of this writing, 93 times the number of reported U.S. deaths to coronavirus.[94]

---

91 "Jameela Jamil reveals she had an abortion when she was young: 'It was the best decision I have ever made'" https://www.yahoo.com/entertainment/jameela-jamil-reveals-she-had-an-abortion-when-she-was-young-it-was-the-best-decision-i-have-ever-made-150616061.html

92 This number was fact-checked in 2015, and was only current through year 2011, and missed numbers from some states for long periods of time. So in reality the true number is likely significantly higher. "FACT CHECK: 50 million abortions claim checks out" https://www.desmoinesregister.com/story/news/politics/reality-check/2015/03/06/million-abortions-claim-checks/24530159/

93 List of US States by Population https://www.nationsonline.org/oneworld/US-states-population.htm

94 Based on 536,000 deaths on March 16th, 2021.

Who knows how many more have occurred throughout the world.

This has been *normalized* here. We almost forget about it at times.

But life-taking is never normalized in God's Kingdom.

There are reasons and justifications galore, but the bottom line is that in our world, sex is one of the foremost idols that is worshipped. We demand to be able to have sex when and where we want with no consequences. Responsibility for a baby that may result is resisted, whether the responsibility for a female to carry and care for it or a male to protect and provide for it.

As is the case with Adam and Eve, passive and foolish males bear much of the responsibility and blame here. Abortion is not a female sin, because it takes male and female to create any life.

But the thing about idols is that they always, always demand a sacrifice. Worship of them requires a sacrifice to be placed on the altar, and it just so happens that the worship of sex demands the sacrifice of the children it creates. We don't place our children in a fiery statue of Molech anymore, but we do subject them to unseen horrors so we won't have to deal with the many restrictions they bring to our lives.

But as Mother Theresa notes, there is great spiritual poverty in this.

"It is a poverty to decide that a child must die so that you may live as you wish."

Mother Theresa

WE CAN'T HEAR THEM CRYING

In the United States and some of the world, abortion is legal, with varying degrees of restriction. Some cities and states are seeking to take away restrictions, such as New York City and Virginia. The impetus there is to remove barriers to women seeking abortions, and broaden the acceptable reasons for post-viability abortions to be increasingly vague. Anything that threatens not just the life, but the broad "health" of the mother, can be seen as justification—and that "health," according to Supreme Court case *Doe v. Bolton*, can include "physical, emotional, psychological, familial, and the woman's age."[95]

95 "Addressing New York's New Abortion Law" https://www.factcheck.org/2019/02/addressing-new-yorks-new-abortion-law/

Which basically means, abortion can be justified at almost any time for almost any reason. This is proof of the generally sensed movement from the "safe, legal and rare" language of Bill Clinton in decades past to the historically bold moves seen today.

Sadly, in our debates over this contentious issue, there is a prominent voice missing: the voice of those it affects the most.

On April 10th, 2020 a story was published in the *Korea Times* about an abortionist in Seoul who was paid $23,000 to perform a late-term abortion. The baby was born alive during the abortion procedure, and proceeded to cry. Instead of caring for the baby who escaped the procedure alive, the doctor placed the baby in a bucket of water to die.[96]

He was sent to prison and had his license revoked, all because he killed the baby a few seconds too late.[97] If those cries would have never happened, the moral outrage of those in the room would not have been tripped. Our culture would follow the same absurd logic. Our consciences have been blinded by self-interest, seared by idolatry, and cannot seem to be awakened because we can't hear the screams of our victims.

But as the nation of Israel learned in Egypt, God always hears the cries of those no one else does. Those lives are precious to Him, and their oppressive treatment will not go unpunished. The sin of murder will either be paid for by the one who committed it, or paid for by the sacrificial blood of Jesus we all need.

Because in whatever form it takes, the taking of human life always attacks the *imago dei*, and always makes God justifiably and righteously angry.

MURDEROUS HEARTS & OUR SANCTUARY CITY

In case you have gotten through the various topics of this chapter and felt relatively unscathed, Jesus may come along and show how you are more guilty than you realized. In the Sermon on the Mount found in Matthew 5-7,

---

96 "Doctor jailed for killing baby who 'burst out crying' during abortion" https://www.koreatimes.co.kr/www/nation/2020/04/113_287707.html

97 Until 2019, abortion in South Korea was illegal exept for a few common exceptions, but rarely prosecuted. Courts abolished the ban in 2019, and new laws are underway. "South Korean Court Strikes Down Decades-Old Abortion Ban" https://www.npr.org/2019/04/12/712281726/south-korean-court-strikes-down-decades-old-abortion-ban

Jesus upends and expands the wisdom of the day. One teaching point He makes is that murder is not simply an action, but proceeds from unresolved anger in the heart.

> *"You have heard that it was said to those of old, 'You shall not murder; and whoever murders will be liable to judgment.'* ₂₂ *But I say to you that everyone who is angry with his brother will be liable to judgment; whoever insults his brother will be liable to the council; and whoever says, 'You fool!' will be liable to the hell of fire."*

Matthew 5:21-22

Jesus goes after the heart issues that lead to life-taking here, and warns us to take our unrighteous anger seriously. He's not saying that anger in your heart and murder are the same thing, but that one leads to the other.

Anger leads to rage, which leads to murder.

Anger leads to attempts to drown its waves with alcohol, which leads to a wreck. Anger reveals the evil of deep-seated racism or prejudice, that leads you to devalue the life of someone who looks different than you.

Anger over an unplanned pregnancy and a derailed life plan leads to considering options you never thought you would.

Anger destroys peace and joy and, eventually, life itself.

Who among us does not possess a murderous heart? One teeming with the seeds that could eventually turn into action, even if they haven't done so yet?

The call for all of us is to repent of unrighteous anger and the devaluing of human life. We all possess varying degrees of guilt in Jesus' expansion of the sixth commandment, but the good news is that Jesus doesn't. He is the one and only perfect Son, who never once succumbed to the rage of unrighteous anger. Instead, He allowed Himself to be killed by an angry mob to buy back our murderous hearts and redeem our murderous actions.

He did all of that so that He could become the refuge we flee to from our sin (Hebrews 6:18). He became the eternal sanctuary city for all who would come to Him who have killed, whether intentionally like Paul or David, unintentionally like the ancient Israelites who fled to sanctuary cities to escape wrath, or only internally so far, in our hearts and imaginations.

If you have been involved in taking a life in any way, know that there is grace for you in the sanctuary of Christ. He took on the wrath you deserve so that you would not have to carry the unbearable weight of it.

Come to Him, rest in Him, for He is the only safe place to flee.

INTERLUDE 9
THE COSTS OF SECULARISM

Ursula Le Guin was a well-known American writer who published many novels, short stories, and essays before her death in 2018. Though non-religious, her writing often explored themes of morality, including one popular short story called *The Ones Who Walk Away from Omelas*.

No direct meaning is implied or stated. But in the introduction she later wrote for the story, she references "the dilemma of the American conscience."

The story paints the fictitious city of Omelas as a radiant, prosperous, paradisiacal place full of music, laughter, and festival. There is no king there—no swords, no slaves, no bombs, no advertising. It is a place with few rules and abounding pleasure.

Le Guin goes on to encourage the reader to add whatever they would like to make Omelas *their* picture of boundless delight. If an orgy would help, she says—add an orgy. Let "the glory of desire be proclaimed upon the gongs, and (a not unimportant point) let the offspring of these delightful rituals be beloved and looked after by all."[98]

One thing she is sure of that does not exist in Omelas, however, is guilt. Because guilt would ruin the ecstasy provided by a perfectly hedonistic, secular society.

This point explains the main twist of the story. Because the happiness of the entire city has an important catch:

All of the joy described depends upon the continual torture of a small child locked in a dark broom closet underneath one of the city's majestic buildings.

---

98 Ursula Le Guin, *The Ones Who Walk Away from Omelas*.

This child is naked, covered in sores, and begs to be let out. He or she is fed a half-bowl of corn meal and grease a day, so malnourished that his belly protrudes, her legs have no calves. Occasionally someone will come in and kick the child to make him stand up, others will peer at her with frightened, disgusted eyes.

They all know it's there. Some have braved the trip to see the child, while others simply know it is there. They all know that it has to be there, and that every thread of the happiness of their city depends "wholly on this child's abominable misery."[99]

Children in Omelas are told about the terms of their city's happiness between the ages of 8 and 12. Those that choose to go see the child experience rage and disgust, wanting to do something for the child, but feel impotent to do so because all of the joy of life in Omelas would disappear immediately if the child was led out into the sunlight, cared for, and loved.

> *"Those are the terms. To exchange all the goodness and grace of every life in Omelas for that single, small improvement: to throw away the happiness of thousands for the chance of the happiness of one: that would be to let guilt within the walls indeed. The terms are strict and absolute; there may not even be a kind word spoken to the child...*

> *Often the young people go home in tears, or in a tearless rage, when they have seen the child and faced this terrible paradox. They may brood over it for weeks or years. But as time goes on they begin to realize that even if the child could be released, it would not get much good of its freedom: a little vague pleasure of warmth and food, no doubt, but little more. It is too degraded and imbecile to know any real joy. It has been afraid too long to ever be free of fear. Its habits are too uncouth for it to respond to humane treatment. Indeed, after so long it would probably be wretched without walls to protect it, and darkness for its eyes, and its own excrement to sit in. The tears at the bitter injustice dry when they begin to perceive the terrible justice of reality, and to accept it...*[100]

The end of the short story tells of a brave few that do not accept the terms of their city. Because their guilt is not allowed in the city, they only have one option: to leave.

---

99 Ibid
100 Ibid

GETTING WHAT YOU WANT HAS A COST

Le Guin is not a Christian and had no stated intent for this story, but even still, it is a poignant picture of something we have discussed throughout this book: the worship of an idol always demands a sacrifice. The worldview of secularism has in many ways gotten what it wants: freedom from authority of any kind, especially divine authority. But as is true so often...

Getting what you want has a cost.

Some readers of this story naturally ask if it is an allegory for abortion, where the sacrifice of unborn children is necessary for the types of lives citizens demand to have. Le Guin has said no such thing, but it could be noteworthy that she is on record as having an illegal abortion before this story was published, and that it was released in 1973, the same year *Roe v. Wade* passed into law.[101]

Regardless of that application, the story hints at a dilemma of the American conscience that goes back to our founding. Historically speaking, we may be the clearest picture of a group of people seeking to create our own utopia, without the intrusion of a king or authority we don't like. "We the people" sought to make our own rules, with the freedom to rule and for some, even to worship God as we pleased.

But it can be easy to forget that all freedoms have a cost, and that is certainly true for the historically rare freedoms we enjoy today. This is perhaps most easily seen in the sacrifices of untold American soldiers we'll never know or read about, who gave their lives to create or defend this country.

But there's a darker side to this as well, because when our forefathers landed on dry land, a surprising twist awaited: there were already people here. Native Americans.

And as time and society progressed in the new world, the European settlers would have to decide what they would or would not do to attain their vision. Would they live humbly alongside the native communities, protecting their culture and way of life, or would they steadily push them out, take their

---

101 Le Guin processed her feelings about abortion in two writings, "The Princess" and "What it Was Like." She argues that it was justified and necessary. "Ursula Le Guin on Abortion: 'The Princess' & 'What It Was Like'" https://www.readingistherapy.com/ursula-le-guin-on-abortion/

land, and decimate their cultural identities? The stories in our history books of Wounded Knee, the Trail of Tears and others tell us the route that was ultimately chosen.

Getting what you want has a cost.

Next, there was the challenge of how to build a country from the ground up. So much work was needed, so boats sailed across the Atlantic to steal innumerable people with darker skin—proclaimed at the time to be sub-human—to force them to do the dirty work. The ones that survived the trip were subjected to generations of unthinkably despicable and inhumane treatment.

Getting what you want has a cost.

In some ways, our country has learned from our past mistakes, though one could certainly argue our response to slavery was not an outright pursuit to right wrongs but more of a half-hearted disavowal of evil and pretending that its effects would disappear without significant restoration. (Freed slaves were promised 40 acres and a mule, but never received this justice—while in some cases former slave owners were compensated for the loss of a slave.)[102]

Even faced with our most grotesque sins and national embarrassments, which still have lingering effects today—we have slowly corrected course and, at least to varying degrees, increasingly become a beacon of hope to the world.

But we would be mistaken to think that abortion doesn't fit perfectly in this frame.

Getting what you want has a cost.

And what our culture wants is to be able to have sex when we want, without any consequences.

---

102 The story behind the promise of "40 acres and a mule" is heartbreaking and poignant. The idea came from a meeting General Sherman had with 20 African American pastors (9 of who were former slaves) where Sherman did what no one had thought to do before: ask the leaders of the black community what they wanted for their people after slavery. Their answer was: land. So they could build and create wealth. Four days later, President Lincoln approved it, but his predecessor Andrew Johnson, a sympathizer with the south, rescinded the order and gave the land back to the planters that owned it: "the very people who declared war on the United States of America." "The Truth Behind '40 Acres and a Mule'" https://www.pbs.org/wnet/african-americans-many-rivers-to-cross/history/the-truth-behind-40-acres-and-a-mule/

Virginia, one of the states seeking to expand abortion rights in recent years, has a state flag that shows a woman with a slain tyrant under her foot, meant to represent the defeat of Great Britain by Virginia.

Below the image lies the Latin phrase *sic semper tyrannis*, which translates to "thus always to tyrants." The saying is attributed to a famous event in Roman history: Marcus Brutus shouted it while he and his co-conspirators killed emperor Julius Caesar.

It also was shouted by John Wilkes Booth after shooting Abraham Lincoln at Ford Theatre, because southerners saw him as a tyrant that kept them from separating from the north over the issue of slavery. As Jonathan Haidt comments on these historical examples: "Murder often seems virtuous to revolutionaries."[103] Sometimes it feels necessary to get what you want.

We've been overthrowing tyrants ever since King George. Sometimes others, like Lincoln, become casualties of the fight. And it just so happens that one of the foremost "tyrants" of today are very small and voiceless children, the fruit of our demand to have sex on our terms.

It's quite uncool in our culture to be an advocate for the unborn. You are painted as a stodgy extremist who must hate women and their autonomy, instead of an incredibly reasonable voice asking painfully obvious questions. That is no surprise, because standing up to other forms of oppression through history was not celebrated either.

OBSERVATIONS ON GOOD, EVIL, & POLITICS

Our nation, like any other, is a mixture of good and evil both historical and present. We are not called to "walk away" from here, because of past or present evil, because if so we would have to leave any country. As Paul says, in order to leave the evil of the world we would have to leave the world itself (1 Corinthians 5:9-10).

---

103 Jonathan Haidt, *The Righteous Mind*, p.202.

But Paul also calls us "to be wise about what is good, and innocent about what is evil" (Romans 16:19). This means we call good "good" wherever we see it, and we call evil "evil" wherever we see it. We can be proud of the many shining points of our country while we mourn and grieve the evil that co-exists with the good. Those are not mutually exclusive. We can love America without over-identifying with America.

"He who accepts evil without protesting against it is really cooperating with it."

Dr. Martin Luther King, Jr.

This call means we throw off any lesser identities or group affiliations that fight to be our foremost lens. We are citizens of this world, but we are *primarily* citizens of another world. We are Christian far before and far more centrally than we are Democrat or Republican, or even American for that matter.

In our imperfect two party system, our political engagement often has to choose the lesser of two evils. Both sides have mixtures of good and evil, and neither holds the vision of human flourishing God has in Scripture.

For some Christians, the unthinkable evil of abortion and the destruction of the nuclear family makes this decision, even when a leader is far from holding the morals they would desire of any leader. For others, concern for the historically oppressed among racial lines, economic inequality, or other concerns take precedent, and they vote for a candidate who is morally deficient in other ways. In both outcomes, many feel they are required to choose the lesser of two evils.

For all of us as Christians, there is potential for great danger when we fall into our political parties like the citizens of Omelas, justifying the bad as a condition for the good and pretending like nothing is wrong. Jesus did not die to make our primary identity red or blue, but to rescue us out of the broken systems of this world into the only true city of eternal flourishing and delight.

That gives us the freedom to call evil evil wherever it is found—and the courage it takes to do so, being beholden to nothing. We must retain prophetic distance, and the ability to vote for someone and still call out the evil they exhibit. If we don't, we are living in Omelas.

We were not made for that fictitious city, but for the shining city in the mountains, purified of all evil—where joy is not contingent upon another's suffering. May we have the courage to pursue the narrow path to that shimmering city, coming down out of heaven from God (Revelation 21:2).

CHAPTER 10
YOU SHALL NOT COMMIT ADULTERY

LOYALTY CARE/HARM

You shall not commit adultery.

Exodus 20:14

The bed's getting cold and you're not here
The future that we hold is so unclear
But I'm not alive until you call
And I'll bet the odds against it all
Save your advice 'cause I won't hear
You might be right but I don't care
There's a million reasons why I should give you up
But the heart wants what it wants
The heart wants what it wants
The heart wants what it wants
The heart wants what it wants

Selena Gomez, *The Heart Wants What it Wants*

WHERE IDEAS COME FROM

In just six words, "the heart wants what it wants" forms a resounding summary of our culture's pursuit of sex outside of any boundaries. Whether spoken or felt, that reasoning has been the golden ticket to free up millions to pursue promiscuity, affairs, pornography addiction, and other acts classified as sexual sin according to Scripture.

Many do not know where the line from the hit song originated from, however, and Selena Gomez may be one of them.

Filmmaker Woody Allen started dating Mia Farrow in 1980. They never married, both having been married twice already, but they did adopt two children and had one biological child together. They lived separately in New York City, and Mia Farrow had an adopted daughter, Soon-Yi Previn, from a previous relationship who was 10 years old when their relationship started.

In the early 1990s, Farrow found nude pictures of Soon-Yi that Allen had taken, exposing the affair that started between Soon-Yi and Woody after she went off to college. He was 35 years older than her—she was the adopted daughter of his girlfriend and the sibling of his own biological and adopted kids.

During a custody battle over the kids in 1993, Allen testified about his relationship with Previn.

"'At the very outset, it didn't occur to me that this would be anything but a private thing,' he said, saying he hadn't really considered how the affair would affect his children. 'I felt nobody in the world would have any idea.'

When the judge asked 'Wasn't that enough, that you would know that you were sleeping with your children's sister?' Allen responded 'I didn't see it that way. I'm sorry.'"[104]

Woody and Soon-Yi would later marry in 1997, and remain together to this day with two adopted children of their own. In a famous interview with Walter Isaacson in Time magazine in 1992, Isaacson pressed him on all of the absurd dynamics of his affair and the heartache it must have caused everyone involved. Allen shares his conclusion in the last line of the interview:

"The heart wants what it wants. There's no logic to those things. You meet someone and you fall in love and that's that."[105]

---

104 "A history of Woody Allen and Soon-Yi Previn describing their relationship, from 'the heart wants what it wants' to 'I was paternal'" https://www.salon.com/2015/07/30/a_history_of_woody_allen_and_soon_yi_previn_describing_their_relationship_from_the_heart_wants_what_it_wants_to_i_was_paternal/

105 "The Heart Wants What It Wants" - TIME http://content.time.com/time/magazine/article/0,9171,160439,00.html

THE DESIGN & THE DECEIT THAT SHATTERS IT

Worlds away from the story mentioned above, we find the biblical vision of sex and marriage scattered from the first to the last pages of Scripture. We see a creation story that involves one man and one woman, equal but different, who are called to be co-creators with God living in covenant with Him and each other. Their devotion and love for one another is life-giving in the most literal way, as the act of their union creates more image bearers to fill the Earth, bow to their Creator and rule over creation.

In this covenantal relationship, lifelong love and service to one another provides a symbiotic joy. No one has to worry if their needs are being met because selflessness reigns, and sex is the physical act that solidifies and continues to renew that covenant. Children are brought into the world to meet the lifelong security of a home where love swirls like oxygen, never doubting that the next breath won't be there.

In this vision, the man and woman do not see their relationship as primarily about them, because they are lost in a view as big as the gospel story that has generational and even eternal effects. The heart's fleeting desires— far from being unquestioned directives to follow at any cost—are seen as untrustworthy and destructive.

> *The heart is deceitful above all things,*
> *and desperately sick;*
> *who can understand it?*
> **Jeremiah 17:9**

The sinful heart leaps after all sorts of things that would destroy it, so who cares what the heart wants? It is meant to be submitted to the higher and deeper desires that breed profound joy. In this act of lifelong submission to God's design, true freedom and countless delights are found.

There are shadows of this design in the purest of love stories, the best of weddings, the rare show or movie whose depiction of a family makes you cry—but only a shadow. The real thing is far better.

At a recent wedding of two Midtown members, the real thing was put on display in the vows of the husband:[106]

---

106 From the wedding of Ryan and Samantha Sanders. Used with permission.

I have lived my life with many wonderful examples of what it means to be a Godly father and husband. The person who stands out the most is my grandpa. He committed his entire life to loving, protecting, and providing for my grandma. Even as my grandma's physical and mental health declined with age he remained present and invested.

When she could not walk, he carried her.

When she could not bathe, he washed her.

When she could not speak, he read to her.

When she could not eat, he fed her.

When she could not breathe, he gave all the air he had to breathe for her.

And through it all he never stopped praying for her.

To think: the heart and its wayward whims could keep us from that?

From the very beginning of time, Satan's deceitful ideas have been attacking the staggering design we see in Scripture. His lies ring out still:

Did God really say sex only belongs in the covenant of marriage?

Why would He say that?

Does He just want you to be miserable?

Does He just want to keep you under His oppressive rule?

Because He knows when you eat that forbidden fruit you'll be like Him... you'll be enlightened?

Those deceitful ideas play to the disordered desires of our flesh, that would prefer sex to be on our terms. And they have most certainly been normalized in our sinful society, as almost any pop song would attest—along with most movies and shows that glorify the thrill of unboundaried sex.

The heart wants what it wants, after all.

And so, like our first grandparents, we bite. And like every form of rebellion, untold destruction awaits.

HARM & SEXUAL SIN

As we have seen from Haidt's experiments on moral dumbfoundedness, it sometimes takes an extreme case to cause moral faculties to awaken and pronounce judgment. The story of Woody Allen's affair with his children's sibling, and the staggering amount of chaos and pain it unleashed, is such an extreme case. It makes almost anyone furrow their brow in confusion and disgust. The absurdity and damage of "the heart wants what it wants" is on full display.

But it does not need to be so extreme to notice the personal and societal damage done by such a premise. If you grew up in a home shattered by infidelity or divorce you know this well. Many endure nasty custody battles, and are shuffled back and forth in chaos when they are meant for stability.

The effects of family breakdown can be devastating even if radically normalized, and can last for generations. But pain is not spared for the one following their heart, either. Contrary to what Satan would suggest, God's forbiddance of adultery is not meant to keep a person unhappy. His boundaries are for our joy and good, always, and the joy and good of our descendants.

The human heart was made for attachment. Deeper joys are found through lifelong relationship, where real people with real sin issues experience costly forgiveness in the context of covenant love. Adultery severs that attachment and the future it promises. It trades the deep for the shallow, the long for the short, and deforms those who commit it spiritually, emotionally, and relationally.

Because adultery is idolatry, and idolatry always causes harm. Whereas the second commandment forbade the worship of created images, adultery is the physical acting out of that false worship. It is the worship of another created in God's image, and it comes with gruesome demands.

We all know this at least to a degree. We all have been touched by the relational and familial harm caused by sexual sin to a certain extent. If you have not lived through it, someone close to you has. When so many marriages and families are broken by this, it becomes normalized.

Add to that normalization the extent to which we are steeped in "follow your heart" messaging, and unfaithfulness becomes a tricky thing. For an American, his or her feelings about an affair very well may change based on who they are friends with: *the one who cheated* ("They were just following their heart, I just want them to be happy...") or *the one cheated on* ("They are the scum of the Earth because they hurt my friend...").

But no amount of justification, and no degree of happinesses found through chasing the desires of the heart will ever erase the destruction it causes, whether seen or unseen.

LOYALTY & SEXUAL SIN

In addition to father/child imagery, one of the most prevalent metaphors for the relationship God intends to have with us is that of marriage. The entire book of Hosea in the Old Testament is one long allegory where God tells Hosea to marry an unfaithful prostitute named Gomer, and put on display how he feels about her whoring herself out to other lovers time and time again. Through his pain we see God's heartache over our continual spiritual adultery, our refusal to live in covenant with Him.

We see that we were designed for faithfulness. Our joy comes alive through attachment to God, but our sin nature continually seeks to sever that attachment. We trade the abiding joy of union with God for the flash of the eyes or the prick of the heart.

In Ephesians 5, Paul tells us that for Christians, there is a mystery put on display through marriage. Christ has made a way for the spiritually unfaithful to be forgiven and restored to relationship with Him, and Christian marriage is to put that faithfulness on display. Adultery is given even more weight, because it lies about God. Our faithfulness is meant to show the world that God is faithful (Ephesians 5:25-33).

In the context of faithfulness and loyalty, sex functions as a test. How do you prove you are faithful to your spouse alone? By having sex with them and them alone. How do you prove that you are faithful to Christ, who purchased your salvation with His own blood? By having sex only in the bounds that He sets, forsaking all sexual expression outside of that.

You can say all day long that you are faithful to your wife, buf if you are acting out the sad trope of sleeping with your secretary, you are a liar. You can claim until you are blue in the face that you follow Jesus, but if you reject His sexual ethic you are no different than Gomer.

This is what is bewildering about theological progressives that claim Christ but reject scriptural boundaries for sex. There is no clearer test for faithfulness in marriage, or in Christ, than whether or not you are willing to submit your sexual desires.

Sex is a test.

JESUS MAKES IT WORSE

It is a common misunderstanding that God in the Old Testament is a bit harsh but then Jesus shows up and is more smooth around the edges. This falsehood is undercut by many things, one of which is the way Jesus actually expands the laws given in the Ten Commandments. You may feel some degree of escape from this command if you have not committed a physical affair while married, but that relief dissolves quickly when faced with these words:

> *"You have heard that it was said, 'You shall not commit adultery.'*
> *28 But I say to you that everyone who looks at a woman with lustful intent has already committed adultery with her in his heart.*

> **Matthew 5:27-28**

To be clear, there is a very meaningful difference between adultery of the heart and the physical act of adultery. Jesus is not equating those things here, but rather showing where the act originates. Unfaithfulness starts in the heart that gives into the whims of its wants. It starts in the mind, in letting down the guard for fantasy, with eyes that don't bounce but linger.

The Greek word for "lustful intent" here is *epithumeo*, which means to desire, to covet, or long for.[107] It is what happens when a sinful heart wants what it wants. Birthed in thoughts that are not taken captive, it leads to fantasy, searching, clicking, self-fulfillment of physical desire or acting out with another. If *epithumeo* is not destroyed by faithfulness, it does the destroying itself.

---

107 Kevin DeYoung, *The Ten Commandments.*

Elsewhere Jesus forbids "sexual immorality" (Mark 7:21-23), a call repeated numerous times through the New Testament. That is the Greek word *porneia*, which is a catch-all term describing sexual activity outside of covenant marriage, from which the word *pornography* is derived.

In the world of secularism, this view of human sexuality is seen as foolish at best, oppressive and harmful at worst.

> *"No commandment prickles more than the seventh. Many live by a creed of sexual autonomy: my body is my own, and my sexual desires, whatever they are, are normal and healthy. How dare the Lord—how dare anyone interfere with my constitutional right to think and do and feel whatever I d*** well please? Can I have a little privacy, please?"*
>
> **Peter Leithart, *The Ten Commandments***

Sex is so elevated here that denial of its desires feels like the worst suffering imaginable. It is often described as a "drive." But it's not.[108] "Drives" are things like hunger and thirst, things that keep you alive. No one has ever died from lack of sex. Jesus was the most fulfilled human that ever lived and He never had sex.

In secularism, the only true parameter around sex is consent. But Yahweh is concerned with far more than that, and He prohibits consensual forms of sex between adults. He steps in on Sinai and the clarifications that would follow, and brings many intrusions on our autonomy and privacy.

He builds a fence around sex much smaller than our culture affirms—and in this case, smaller is better. Sexual desire has been likened to a fire, and marriage is the perfect container for it to burn. When sex gets outside of that, it burns things down.

IMAGE BEARERS, NOT ANIMALS

God is restrictive about sex, not because He is a prude. He created it after all. He formed the chemicals and synapses that make it so enjoyable. He made it an act that combines intense pleasure with deep relational meaning, to form an attachment or even addiction to one another. Where a husband and wife keep coming back to one another's arms, and only their arms, for good.

---

108 "Sex Drive? There's No Such Thing" https://www.psychologytoday.com/us/blog/living-single/201504/sex-drive-theres-no-such-thing

He is restrictive about sex because, again, He has a higher view of humanity than our culture does. Culture essentially says we are glorified animals with insatiable drives, unleashed to pursue them as long as we have consent. God knows that such an approach belittles sex and debases those who participate in it. He did not create us to be animals, but raised us above them. In having dominion over them, we are to have dominion over the desires that feel animalistic to us.

He intends for us to be co-creators and co-rulers with Him in a lifelong covenant that is for our good, the good of our children, the good of society, and the good of the world. A God-honoring marriage tells the truth about God.

He is faithful, merciful, and complete. He is trustworthy to properly fill the desires He created. He is patient as He calls us back to the flourishing we were made for, but He does call us back. We were made for more than the chaos and destruction of chasing the deceitful desires of our hearts.

He is not trying to keep us down, like Satan and culture says. *He is trying to raise us up.*

A Father who is always for our good—He is teaching us how to live in His house.

INTERLUDE 10
THE FUTURE OF SECULARISM

In an article called "Resisting the Spirit of the Age," theologian and pastor Carl Trueman argues that "freedom," as our culture defines it, has become the primary deity we worship. Secularism demands that no true God reign over us and boss us around with dictates. Kings are not welcome here, and authority is always suspect.

This freedom has many, many benefits. But also some costs. Trueman writes:

> *"The trouble is that the tame gods we invent to serve us never stay tame for long. We hoped they would serve us, but we end up serving them. And so it is with the idolizing of 'freedom.' As time has gone on, it has demanded greater and greater sacrifices of those who worship it. It has demanded the end of moral norms on sexual behavior, the right to kill our children, and the destruction of marriage. It demands the silencing of those who don't agree with its demands. Right now, it is demanding the freedom to define who we are even in the face of the scientific realities of male and female, thus demanding that we give up on the very possibility of objective truth. And, of course, it will not stop there."*[109]

His point is worth considering. As our culture moves farther towards a post-Christian, post-objective-truth, secular end—the demands of freedom will intensify.

Christian doctors in some fields already face difficult conundrums around the area of gender dysphoria, as do Christian professionals in the mental health field. What does one do in a culture that has moved past reality

---

109 "Resisting the Spirit of the Age" https://tabletalkmagazine.com/article/2018/03/resisting-spirit-age/

itself and where the superiors and authorities in your field encourage or mandate that you participate in unreality?

Pastors and churches still have robust protections under freedom of religion, but Trueman ponders what the future could hold. What will we do in the face of increased, morally-framed pressure to reject a biblical sex ethic? Or when we are pressed to refer to people by an ever-expanding list of non-binary gender pronouns? Is there a time coming where orthodox Christian belief may be considered widely, if not legally, as intolerant hate speech? Trueman chimes in again:

> *"But doesn't 'freedom' enable us as Christians to believe what we want without persecution? Not when it is treated as an ultimate good. For then it only grants permission for Christians to worship our God provided we accept that 'freedom' is the truly fundamental thing, that the worship of the Holy Trinity is optional while adherence to the doctrines of 'freedom' are not. In other words, it will protect Christianity only so long as we accord our God second place in the divine pantheon. 'Freedom' lays claim to the first.*
>
> *For that reason, it is only a matter of time before this secular religion, far from guaranteeing the right to worship the Christian God, will in the end forbid it. For 'freedom' requires what God forbids and vice versa. Faithfulness to Jesus Christ means defying this deity when it demands that we sign up ourselves and our children for its morality and its mantras. Idols, in the end, can tolerate subordinates but not rivals. The deity of 'freedom' will no more be an exception than was Caesar in the days of the New Testament."[110]*

To be clear, this is a potential prophecy, not a reality. We are not fully to these conclusions yet, by any means. But when viewed as a spirit and a trajectory, it's not at all crazy to consider.

"Idols, in the end, can tolerate subordinates but not rivals." That is undeniably true when one looks at Scripture. We will not worship both freedom and God, so what will happen as our culture increasingly demands that we "sign up ourselves and our children for its morality and mantras?"

What should happen is what has happened through history when faithful Christians have faced similar ultimatums.

---

110 Ibid

We pick up our cross and follow Jesus, no matter what hardship may come.

We lock our eyes on a heavenly city in a distant country, not deformed by unreality or run by idols.

We pledge citizenship to our eternal home, no matter the cost.

CHAPTER 11
YOU SHALL NOT STEAL

FAIRNESS

You shall not steal.

Exodus 20:15

"'Thou shalt not steal' is a character description of Jesus, and obedience to this command is obedience to the gospel, the call to imitate Jesus' labor and self-gift."

Peter Leithart, *The Ten Commandments*

ENTER THE FOUNDATION OF FAIRNESS

In the eighth commandment, the voice of Sinai booms with a resounding truth: God cares about the treatment of His image bearers. As anyone who has ever been stolen from knows, the bubbling anger that follows the intrusive and demeaning act points to design: *how does someone get off treating me this way?*

As with all the commandments, the umbrella includes much more underneath it. Consider the context of the Israelites: *they* had just been stolen by the Egyptians. It is not just things that can be stolen, but people too. Lives and families can be stolen in slavery, bodily safety stolen in sexual assault, dignity stolen through mistreatment. When Paul recounts the deeds of those who break the second table of commandments in 1 Timothy, he lists those that break this commandment as "enslavers" (1 Timothy 1:8-11).

Just one chapter after the Ten Commandments are given in Exodus 20, God says the penalty for human stealing and selling is death (Exodus 21:16). If those who stole humans from Africa and brought them in ships to the New World had lived in ancient Israel, they wouldn't have lived long.[111]

---

111 Instances of slavery found in the Bible were generally far less severe than the chattel slavery of early America and more like indentured servitude.

In Exodus 22, God gives another dire warning to His gathered people, warning them to not treat others the way they'd been treated in Egypt:

You shall not wrong a sojourner or oppress him, for you were sojourners in the land of Egypt. ₂₂ You shall not mistreat any widow or fatherless child. ₂₃ If you do mistreat them, and they cry out to me, I will surely hear their cry, ₂₄ and my wrath will burn, and I will kill you with the sword, and your wives shall become widows and your children fatherless.

Exodus 22:21-24

If you ever wonder whether God cares for the vulnerable or the oppressed, the sojourner or widow or orphan—it doesn't get much clearer than "I will kill you with the sword, and *your* wives shall become widows and *your* children fatherless." No ambiguity there.

In the following verses, we see God's heart for the poor, and those who would take advantage of their plight to make money:

If you lend money to any of my people with you who is poor, you shall not be like a moneylender to him, and you shall not exact interest from him. ₂₆ If ever you take your neighbor's cloak in pledge, you shall return it to him before the sun goes down, ₂₇ for that is his only covering, and it is his cloak for his body; in what else shall he sleep? And if he cries to me, I will hear, for I am compassionate.

Exodus 22:25-27

What a beautiful picture that is, that the God enthroned in the heavens would think, "Is that poor man going to be cold tonight?" He is compassionate, so He hears. The truth that God cares about how His image bearers are treated doesn't stop here but carries on, from the leaving of edges of your field to be gleaned by the poor (Leviticus 23:22), to the call to care for widows and orphans from Jesus' brother (James 1:27).

It is a good thing not to take something that is not yours, as is emphasized in this commandment. But the ethical vision built off of it also includes considering those who have had things taken from them through injustice, suffering, or poverty. As always, Jesus is our model here, who not only did not take what did not belong to Him, but gave up what did belong to Him for us.

A THEOLOGY OF THINGS

Consider a real-life nightmare: what if you woke up to find yourself in one of those all-white rooms seen in the movies. Nothing around you but walls, a floor, and a ceiling. There is oxygen pumping in, but no hope of anything else.

How long would you last?

A machine would be fine in there forever. Not so with you. Without food, water, or an iPhone to call for help, you have a matter of days.

Because you are a *creature*. Which means you need—are absolutely dependent upon—*things*. On food, water, shelter, clothing, money to buy all of those very necessary resources.

This is not negative—it's how God designed us. Jesus Himself spent money at the market to buy food and enjoyed the warmth of clothing and covering at night. Jesus is not against possessions—He's against our over-attachment and worship of them.

Because we are creatures, the things we rely on to keep us alive and safe in a way, become part of us.[112] They are so meaningful because they give our lives security and shape. Think not only of the money that buys your food or the roof that keeps you dry, but of the things you would run to grab if your home caught on fire. A child may have a well-loved stuffed animal that has been with her through thick-and-thin, and adult creatures do not altogether grow out of that.

So when your things get stolen or destroyed, it hurts. Because they belong to a creature God loves, who needs at least some things to survive.

THE ORIGINAL THIEVES

God created Adam and Eve to have dominion. To have delegated authority over creation and take responsibility for the flourishing of all entrusted to them. And there was much entrusted, as is reflected in the string of "everys" found at the end of Genesis 1.

> *And God said, "Behold, I have given you every plant yielding seed that is on the face of all the earth, and every tree with seed in its fruit. You shall have them for food. 30 And to every beast of the earth and to every bird of the heavens and to everything that*

---

112 Peter Leithart, *The Ten Commandments*.

creeps on the earth, everything that has the breath of life, I have given every green plant for food." And it was so.

Genesis 1:29-30

These creatures were called to take care of the plants, animals, and Earth they would need to survive, a robust responsibility that would keep them busy for life. But they weren't satisfied with exercising their rule over innumerable creatures and creations. They wanted the one and only thing God said was His alone: the tree of the knowledge of good and evil. They were deceived, and they stole from God.[113] God knows the feeling of violation we feel when stolen from, because He was stolen from too.

So the call from Sinai, again, is a reversal of the Garden of Eden. It's a reprimand that in God's house, we do not take what is not ours to take. We respect and dignify one another. It forbids the many forms of stealing we have been committing since the first theft long ago.

STEALING THROUGH GREED

Our first thoughts about stealing tend to land on the most obvious kind: when someone, like Adam and Eve, greedily reaches out their hands to take what isn't theirs. This can be proactive and obvious, as in the clear theft of resources from another person, business, or entity.

In the civil laws of ancient Israel, such thefts were to be repaid with restitution. In the case of money or goods, the stolen amounts were repaid double—in the case of oxen or sheep, they were repaid 5 times the stolen amount (Exodus 22:1-14). Rather than simply serving jail time or a "debt to society," this system allowed the owner to actually get his or her resources back (and then some) to offset the injustice. Speaking on this system of restitution, Leithart notes a helpful point:

"This is preferable to imprisonment. If I go to prison for stealing $100, the victim never gets his $100 back, and I pay far more than $100 in time, loss of reputation, despair, criminalization. I pay "debt to society," but I never pay what I owe to the victim. Restitution punishes the criminal in proportion to his crime and protects the rights of victims."[114]

---

113 Ibid
114 Peter Leithart, *The Ten Commandments*. Footnote 101.

This logic of restitution drives the long-discussed topic of reparations for African Americans descended from the slave trade. Although slaves were freed, no form of monetary restitution was ever given to them. Many were promised "40 acres and a mule" along the South Carolina, Georgia, and Florida coasts—but never got it. Many thousands went to live on the land promised to them, only to have it taken from them and given back to the planters who originally owned the land after Lincoln was killed.[115] Extreme poverty forced former slaves to stay in slave-like conditions, and those effects would not disappear quickly through generations.[116]

In the civil laws of ancient Israel, when wrongs *can* be righted, they *are* to be righted. This restitution seeks after justice, and re-affirms the dignity of the one wronged or stolen from.

If upon reading this you were to feel good about not being imprisoned for grand theft or participating in historical injustices, the wide examples of theft through greed may change that. The Heidelberg Catechism gives a robust explanation of what is forbidden by this command:

"He forbids not only outright theft and robbery, punishable by law. But in God's sight theft also includes cheating and swindling our neighbor by schemes made to appear legitimate, such as: inaccurate measurements of weight, size, or volume; fraudulent merchandising; counterfeit money; excessive interest; or any other means forbidden by God. In addition he forbids all greed and pointless squandering of his gifts."

- *Cheating and swindling your neighbor through schemes.* Maybe in trying to sell something for more than it's worth, or lying about the condition.

- *Inaccurate measurements*, which is an Old Testament form of unfairness. When business transactions literally took place on scales, it was possible to tip scales in your favor, or even shave off gold or silver from currency to keep while still getting the same value out of it in a transaction.

---

115 "The Truth Behind '40 Acres and a Mule'" https://www.pbs.org/wnet/african-americans-many-rivers-to-cross/history/the-truth-behind-40-acres-and-a-mule/
116 In 2016, the Brookings Institute found the average net worth of a white family was $171,000, compared to the average of $17,150 for black families. This is seen by many as a generational effect not only of slavery, but other injustices from Jim Crow laws to redlining. "Examining the Black-white wealth gap" https://www.brookings.edu/blog/up-front/2020/02/27/examining-the-black-white-wealth-gap/

- *Fraudulent merchandising*, which certainly could include forms of manipulative advertising common in our culture.

- *Counterfeit money or excessive interest*, which forms a category for unfair business practices.

Add to that *greed and pointless squandering of his gifts*, and well, who of us would escape?

In our world things grow more complex when you consider piracy of movies and music that you did not pay for but feel justified in taking, fudging on your taxes to cheat the government you don't care about wronging, or plagiarizing someone else's content without attribution.

It would certainly include cheating workers out of their rightful wages, or taking advantage of the poor that don't know how to get what is rightfully theirs. The brother of Jesus chimes in with strong words for those who conduct business with fraud or deceit:

> *Behold, the wages of the laborers who mowed your fields, which you kept back by fraud, are crying out against you, and the cries of the harvesters have reached the ears of the Lord of hosts.*

James 5:4

Consider insurance fraud, tax evasion, or those who swoop in to get rich off of someone else's misfortune.

Another weighty consideration is that in the Old Testament, God declared that those refusing to tithe were actually robbing *Him*. In Malachi 3, God bluntly calls out His people for their lack of obedience in generosity, and even connects it to a curse (Malachi 3:8-10). He goes on to challenge them to "bring the full tithe into the storehouse," to see if He would not rain down blessings until there is no need.

The goal of all of the warnings of greed is for us to be content with what we have. The bar is not simply to refrain from walking into your neighbor's house to take something, but to have a heart that doesn't want to—because you are radically content with what God has provided for you. This picture of contentment is compelling and beautiful, and also challenging for most any American.

THE CHALLENGE OF CONTENTMENT IN AMERICA

A documentary called *The Century of the Self* perhaps explains the American difficulty with contentment better than anything else. It shows examples of advertisements from before WW1, which were mostly utilitarian in nature. They were essentially: *"Did your shoes break? Look, we make new shoes." "Hey, is your car shot? Lucky for you, we make new cars that last a long time."*

And then came a man named Edward Bernays, who was actually the nephew of Sigmund Freud. He studied his uncle's insights to determine what makes people do the things they do, deciding, in his words, that "If you could use propaganda for war, you can certainly use it for peace."[117] The documentary claims that though virtually unknown today, the influence of Bernays was almost as great as his uncle's—because he was the first person to show companies how to manipulate the masses to want things they didn't need.

Corporations were mass-producing goods, and were terrified that people would eventually have enough and stop buying what they were mass-producing. They realized that in order to profit, they would need to transform the mind of the masses to buy based on *want* rather than *need*. Bernays' solution to this problem was simple: to tie a *product*—like a new car, to a *desire*—to be admired and respected.

Smoking was taboo for women at the time, and Bernays was approached by a tobacco executive who asked how they could tap into half the market they were essentially missing. Bernays formulated a plan: he persuaded a group of female debutants to join a NYC parade and at his command, dramatically light cigarettes. Meanwhile, he told the press there were a group of suffragettes who were lighting "torches of freedom," symbolizing their freedom from oppression. The photo op went old-school viral in newspapers, and sales of cigarettes to women skyrocketed.

He simply tied a *product*—cigarettes, to a deeper, subconscious *desire*—freedom, power, and independence.

---

117 The Century of the Self - Part 1: "Happiness Machines" https://www.youtube.com/watch?v=D-nPmg0R1M04

"It made him realize that it was possible to persuade people to behave irrationally if you link products to their emotional desires and feelings. The idea that smoking actually made women freer was completely irrational, but it made them feel more independent."[118]

One of the more disturbing examples shows the impact he had on the fashion world. He sought to tie a *product*—attire, to a *desire*—to express your inner sense of self. A female celebrity from that time is shown, in what would now be considered an overtly drab outfit—plain white shirt, dark skirt, and hat. She appears on grainy black and white film, talking about "the psychology of dress."

She says, *"You all have interesting characters, but some of 'um are all hidden. I wonder why you all want to dress always the same, with the same hats, and the same coats. I'm sure all of you are interesting and have wonderful things about you, but looking at you in the street, you all look so much the same...Try and express yourselves."*[119]

When watching this documentary, the feeling that "we got duped" is overwhelming. People we have never even heard of have shaped our desires in profound ways, that all work to keep us from being content with what God has given us. No wonder radical contentment and rejection of greed is so hard for us!

Ironically, what all those deeply ingrained ideas do is actually steal the joy of contentment from us.

STEALING THROUGH LAZINESS

The Bible has another category for stealing, however, that's less obvious. It's seen through passages like the following:

> *...aspire to live quietly, and to mind your own affairs, and to work with your hands, as we instructed you, 12 so that you may walk properly before outsiders and be dependent on no one.*

> **1 Thessalonians 4:11-12**

Here we see that part of our witness to those outside the faith is that we work hard to provide for ourselves, so we aren't dependent on others if at all possible.

---

118 Ibid
119 Ibid

For even when we were with you, we would give you this command: If anyone is not willing to work, let him not eat. 11 For we hear that some among you walk in idleness, not busy at work, but busybodies. 12 Now such persons we command and encourage in the Lord Jesus Christ to do their work quietly and to earn their own living.

2 Thessalonians 3:10-12

The same is said here, with a stronger caveat: he who won't work shouldn't eat. We've already covered the category of those who truly cannot work or provide for themselves, such as widows, orphans, the disabled, etc. But God's design is that anyone who can work absolutely should. Further reasoning for all of this is given by Paul in Ephesians 4:

Let the thief no longer steal, but rather let him labor, doing honest work with his own hands, so that he may have something to share with anyone in need.

Ephesians 4:28

In this view, lazy people benefit from the hard work of others. They are the grown up versions of the high school group project slackers—they contribute nothing, and still get rewarded through the hard work of others. Some truly need a safety net built by others to survive, but others rely on it when they should be working to provide for themselves, which in a way is stealing from everyone.

Paul says "Let the thief no longer steal," but work so that he can have something to share with others in need. That is the call of redeemed sons and daughters. We don't reject our call to have dominion over this world, but accept it through hard work, so we'll have something for those truly in need.

THE ONE WHO HUNG BETWEEN THIEVES

The biblical story started with thieves in the Garden, and the climactic moment is also surrounded by two thieves.[120] On both sides of Jesus' cross were two notorious stealers and criminals. One made fun of Him, the other asked for grace and had a lifetime of thieving forgiven, finding Himself in paradise the very day he physically paid for his sins on his cross.

---

120 Kevin DeYoung, *The Ten Commandments.*

This unthinkable act Jesus submitted to frames the entire story of creation: He died to turn thieves into sons and daughters.

As the church begins, we see that those sons and daughters followed in the footsteps of their generous Savior. They come together in Acts 2, and what was one of the first acts of Spirit-filled believers? They brought their possessions, the very things needed by creatures to survive, and sold them for those in need.

The opposite of stealing. The undoing of the Garden.

Because that is what we do in the Father's house.

INTERLUDE 11
GOD IS INTRUSIVE (FOR YOUR JOY)

"Unlike the permissive gods of antiquity and modernity, the God of Sinai is an intrusive God who won't leave us alone. He tells Israel that they must worship and serve him alone. He tells them how to worship him, without images. Ever the divine Micromanager, he schedules their week. Ever the divine Idealist, he expects us to live in the real world without violence and vengeance. In the tenth commandment, he really steps over the line and intrudes on thoughts and desires."

Peter Leithart, *The Ten Commandments*

Someone who hates us showed up in a Garden and told us the most insidious lie:

Obedience makes you miserable.

Authority is just to keep you down. God can't be trusted. He's not for your good.

We believed it!

We *believe* it.

Ever since, a preceding Voice has been stepping in. Saying the exact opposite. He showed up to Abram and pointed to the stars. He showed up in Egypt, and in the thick smoke of Mount Sinai. He keeps initiating, rescuing, poking, prodding.

In the ultimate appearance, He showed up in a manger. On the roads and at the tables of first century Israel. On a cross. On a beach, with breakfast.

On the road to Emmaus.

At Pentecost.

He keeps showing up, keeps catching, demanding, our attention. Offering grace and a way back home.

But He is not a tame, spineless God. Not a Father who doesn't care what His kids are like, not a Husband who doesn't care what His wife does when He's not looking.

So with His grace comes law. Always after grace. The Exodus always comes before Sinai.

But Sinai comes, the New Testament comes, and with His grace come His gracious intrusions.

On what we can say, what we can do and not do. On what to do with our wallets and our time. On who we can marry, who we can sleep with (and when). Even what to do with our thoughts, and the vileness found deep in our hearts.

His intrusions are as far-reaching as His grace, it seems. And for a post-Christian world, for secularism—well, we don't do intrusions. We are autonomous. Self-rulers.

We don't do Kings here, and God's intrusions are unthinkable. Unacceptable. Oppressive and maybe even *evil*.

The ever-intrusive God, and His grace are not welcome here. We do not need saving, after all. We've saved ourselves from every tyrant imaginable.

Except for, well—one tyrant we don't often consider the one that looks at us in the mirror. The one that has lied to us more than we know, who thinks she knows what she wants but can't keep the burning questions from rising in the most lonely moments.

Which voice in the Garden was right?

Which voice has my best interest in mind? The one that tells me freedom is found in what I want, or the one that says freedom is found in what He designed?

You would not be the first person to ask that question. The Israelites did so too, with their constant wavering well-known to most of us. At the end of the book of Deuteronomy, where God reiterates all of His laws through Moses, He gives utter clarity to their wandering hearts.

Chapter 28 is a tour-de-force of God's blessings for obedience, along with the curses that will result from disobedience. It is a jarring read that forms a resounding answer to the question "Who is lying: God or Satan?" In this telling, blessings of every kind follow those who listen to Yahweh, the good life truly follows. On the other side, unthinkable curses and anti-good things follow those who reject God's authority.

It's a prophecy, but also just a statement of reality: Life in God's house is good. Life outside, not so much.

God is for our good, the other voice is not.

God ends the book with a crystal clear call:

> "For this commandment that I command you today is not too hard for you, neither is it far off. ₁₂ It is not in heaven, that you should say, 'Who will ascend to heaven for us and bring it to us, that we may hear it and do it?' ₁₃ Neither is it beyond the sea, that you should say, 'Who will go over the sea for us and bring it to us, that we may hear it and do it?' ₁₄ But the word is very near you. It is in your mouth and in your heart, so that you can do it.

> ₁₅ "See, I have set before you today life and good, death and evil. ₁₆ If you obey the commandments of the Lord your God that I command you today, by loving the Lord your God, by walking in his ways, and by keeping his commandments and his statutes and his rules, then you shall live and multiply, and the Lord your God will bless you in the land that you are entering to take possession of it. ₁₇ But if your heart turns away, and you will not hear, but are drawn away to worship other gods and serve them, ₁₈ I declare to you today, that you shall surely perish. You shall not live long in the land that you are going over the Jordan to enter and possess. ₁₉ I call heaven and earth to witness against you today, that I have set before you life and death, blessing and curse. Therefore choose life, that you and your offspring may live, ₂₀ loving the Lord your God, obeying his voice and holding fast to him, for he is your life and length of days, that you may dwell in the land that the Lord swore to your fathers, to Abraham, to Isaac, and to Jacob, to give them."

Deuteronomy 30:11-20

He is your life and length of days. It would be unwise to reject Him.

There is an interesting correlation to this passage at the very end of the Bible, in the book of Revelation. There we see a picture of two cities: Babylon, the great harlot who rejects God in all of her whoring ways, and the New Jerusalem, coming down out of heaven in splendor.

One rejects God, and meets a fiery demise. The other chooses life under God's gracious rule, and eternal blessings follow.

This is the end for us all. The Garden we rejected will turn into a city of one kind or another.

There is a city full of rebellion, haughty pride, and fornication, whose end is an eternal curse.

And one of radiant light emanating from Christ, with trees whose leaves heal the nations in eternal blessing.

Yahweh's words ring out to us still:

I have set before you today life and good, death and evil...

Choose life.

CHAPTER 12
YOU SHALL NOT BEAR FALSE WITNESS AGAINST YOUR NEIGHBOR

FAIRNESS CARE/HARM

You shall not bear false witness against your neighbor.

Exodus 20:16

"Viable human community depends on truth telling...what this commandment is getting at is the public portrayal of reality."

Dave Lomas

THE WORST FORM OF A COMMON SIN

The ninth commandment is often understood as "do not lie," which certainly covers the gist. But the immediate context is a bit more specific, with numerous implications spiraling out from its center as usual. The Hebrew word for *bear* is often translated as "answer," and has courtroom connotations. You answer a summons from a court or judge, and are asked about what you saw your neighbor do or not do.

In the ancient world, witnesses were everything. There were no security tapes, no DNA evidence, no cell phone records.[121] There were only eyes. In ancient Israel, one witness wasn't enough to put someone to death for a capital crime, but two witnesses were enough (Deuteronomy 17:6). The testimony of others bore tremendous weight in life or death matters.

This was exploited in the case of Naboth, whose vineyard was desired by King Ahab and his wife Jezebel in 1 Kings 21. Ahab bartered for the vineyard, but Naboth refused. So Ahab and his wife Jezebel held a banquet and placed two schemers on Naboth's right and left. At once, they stood up and both claimed that he cursed God and the king, crimes punishable by death. He was put to death on the spot, and they took the vineyard.

So we see, like others, that the ninth commandment forbids the worst kind of a particular sin. Just as murder is the worst kind of hatred, adultery the worst kind of lust—bearing false witness about your neighbor was the worst kind of lying. Because it could literally cost someone their life.

It is radically unfair and harmful, as anyone who has been lied about can attest. False testimony is character assassination even if it doesn't assassinate a life.

Consider the viral video captured in May 2020 of Amie Cooper, a white lady in New York City, calling the cops to lie about Christian Cooper, a black man who asked her to leash her dog (a law in Central Park). In her racist, entirely fabricated and hysterical account she weaponizes race relations to bear false witness about a fellow image bearer—accusing an innocent man of endangering her life. One can easily see the damage and character assassination that could have easily followed, and as painful as it is to watch, it's far more painful to live through.

Frankly, it's scary to think about the harm that has been done throughout history by false witness without smartphones to record the lies.

WITNESSES TO TRUTH OR UNREALITY

The extreme and obvious case of lying on the witness stand points to a deeper truth: if we don't tell the truth, devastating chaos and injustices follow. Lies destroy people, relationships, families, communities, even nations and societies. They break the fabric of anything they touch.

Lies are maddening. If you've ever been in a relationship with a habitual liar, or read a novel written with an unreliable narrator, you saw a small picture of this. What do you do when you have no idea if what you're hearing is the truth or not? How does any sort of trust ensue?

When someone lies, they create an alternate world—an *unreality*. The truth is forsaken and the alternate world is created in order to get something they want.

As anyone with kids knows, you don't have to teach them how to do this. Lying and manipulation come as naturally to sinners as breathing. To get something we want, we will gladly participate in *unreality*—we will lie and say our sister did it, fudge the truth and create an alternate world.

When parents get their kids to fess up, they are teaching them to live in reality. They know the unreality of lies leads to chaos and evil, so they lovingly force them back. This is what God is doing on a grand scale at Sinai.

Lying is a small scale acting out of our origin story—Adam & Eve hiding from God in their alternate world, lying to Him and pretending that all was well. Our lying mimics not only their lying, but the first liar, whom Jesus calls the father of lies. Every lie is ultimately traced back to him, and he seeks to use them to kill, steal, and destroy (John 8:39-47, John 10:10).

Lies plunged His image bearers into painful darkness where no one could trust anyone, and everyone had to watch their back from even their brother. The disorienting chaos of Egypt followed, and on the mountain God said "You will no longer live in unreality."

Alternate worlds are not welcome in God's house, so lies will not be spoken by His children. God's people will be witnesses to the truth, agents in recreating the peace it brings.

THE TENDRILS OF A LIE

Climbing out of the soil like a vine, the various ways one can lie multiply. Again here, the Heidelberg Catechism is helpful to understand what this command prohibits:

> *"That I never give false testimony against anyone, twist no one's words, not gossip or slander, nor join in condemning anyone rashly or without a hearing. Rather, in court and everywhere else, I should avoid lying and deceit of every kind; these are the very devices the devil uses, and they would call down on me God's intense wrath. I should love the truth, speak it candidly, and openly acknowledge it. And I should do what I can to guard and advance my neighbor's good name."*

Not twisting words. Not participating in gossip, slander, or condemning without a hearing. Doing everything we can to guard and advance our neighbor's good name. That is a far more robust vision than what you do if you are summoned to court, and the pages of Scripture certainly support it. In the book of Proverbs, our words and the power they have to build up or tear down is a common theme. Consider just a few verses from one chapter, Proverbs 18:

> *A fool takes no pleasure in understanding,*
> *   but only in expressing his opinion.*
> *The words of a whisperer are like delicious morsels;*
> *   they go down into the inner parts of the body.*
> *If one gives an answer before he hears,*
> *   it is his folly and shame.*
> *The one who states his case first seems right,*
> *   until the other comes and examines him.*
> *Death and life are in the power of the tongue,*
> *   and those who love it will eat its fruits.*

Proverbs 18:2, 8, 13, 17, 21

In the New Testament, James brings thunder on how much damage the deceit of our tongues bring:

> *How great a forest is set ablaze by such a small fire! 6 And the tongue is a fire, a world of unrighteousness. The tongue is set among our members, staining the whole body, setting on fire the entire course of life, and set on fire by hell. 7 For every kind of beast and bird, of reptile and sea creature, can be tamed and has been tamed by mankind, 8 but no human being can tame the tongue. It is a restless evil, full of deadly poison.*

James 3:5-8

When speaking of the evil that comes out of our hearts, one of the things Jesus lists is slander, or untrue speech about another (Matthew 15:19-20). Paul calls out gossip (2 Corinthians 12:20, 1 Timothy 5:13). In a worldview of grace, some of Paul's harshest words are for those who stir up divisions with their words:

> *"As for a person who stirs up division, after warning him once and then twice, have nothing more to do with him,"*

Titus 3:10

There is no ambiguity in Scripture: our words either align fully with truth and reality, and therefore build up flourishing—or they align with lies and unreality to bring ruin and chaos. It is not just the big, obvious lies that do this, but the ones hidden in social convention and acceptability.

Gossip is "passing along a report or rumor that cannot be substantiated," or even passing along a true report in ways that are unnecessary and damaging to the person.[122] It bears false witness against someone with juicy rumors that are fun to spread. There may be no cheaper and quicker way to connect with someone than passing on tidbits you know they would enjoy. Gossip is normalized in our culture, and can be accepted even in Christian circles even though it is categorically called sinful in Scripture. Because it tears down the good name of our neighbors—their expense becomes our gain.

It can feel harmless to listen to gossip even if you're not the one spreading it, but listening is participating. The normalization of it can be seen in this dynamic: What if, in the midst of a conversation among Christians that is leaning toward gossip, one voiced up and said "You know what? I don't know if we should be having this conversation. This feels like it is getting too close to gossip..."? Would that feel incredibly normal to you, or a little weird? If you answered weird, that may prove that gossip is normalized and not routinely called out as sinful.

Slander takes it further, in that it is deliberately passing along information that is false. As DeYoung writes, "Sometimes we make mistakes and pass along information that proves inaccurate. But too often we are quick to pass along unsubstantiated, false reports. That's slander."[123]

Slander assassinates the character of its victim, leaving a wake of potentially irrevocable destruction in its path. It breaks down relationships and societies. And a big problem is, sometimes we believe things to be true that are not true at all, and pass that believed-but-untrue information along to others.

---

122 Kevin DeYoung, *The Ten Commandments*.
123 Ibid

SLANDER BY CONDEMNING WITHOUT A HEARING

Martin Luther said that observing the ninth commandment requires us to put "the best construction on everything." Meaning, we give the benefit of the doubt. If a friend doesn't text us back, or is late for a meeting, or another similar situation happens: we assume the best until the worst is proven. (And even if the worst is proven, we confront, forgive, and reconcile.)

This is why the Heidelberg Catechism includes "condemning without a hearing" as a form of breaking this commandment. We are prone to jump to conclusions about situations and people. We think through the lens of stories, so when we see data points in a relationship, we quickly craft a story that makes sense of them:

He must be mad at me because of that thing I said a few weeks ago.
She must be upset with me because I forgot to text her on her birthday last month.
I know exactly why he or she did _____.

In psychological terms, this is called mind reading. It's listed as a cognitive distortion we participate in, and "distortion" is an apt term, because what it often distorts is reality itself. (For more on cognitive distortions, see Appendix 2: Cognitive Distortions.)

One pastor told a fascinating, but understandable story of how this happened to him:[124] One Sunday a church member was walking past the communion table and bumped into it, evidently spilling some of its contents. In the member's version of the story, the pastor locked eyes with him at that moment, judging his recklessness, and embarrassing him. The next Sunday Gathering the member attended, the communion table was moved to a different spot, and the pastor never addressed it with him.

Months later, the member approached the pastor and explained the reason why he had been distant from him in harbored bitterness. He recounted the story and the hurt he had over the pastor's nasty look and the lack of follow up. The pastor's response surprised him:

I have no idea what you are talking about.

---

124 This story and some of the concepts of mind reading as breaking the ninth commandment were shared in this sermon by Dave Lomas: The Stories We Tell Ourselves. https://podcasts.apple.com/us/podcast/bridgetown-audio-podcast/id84246334?i=1000446738625

The pastor went on to explain that he didn't remember him bumping the communion table, didn't remember looking at him, and that communion was moved for another reason entirely.

That brand of chaos is exactly what mind reading and assumptions bring to relationships. When you make up stories based on data points that make sense to you, but are not clearly checked with others, this is what happens. And it is especially tempting to do when you feel hurt by someone, which is unavoidable in relationships.

Now, imagine the enormous harm that is done when this happens in a marriage.

A friendship.

A family.

A LifeGroup.

A church.

Imagine the hell unleashed when these are widespread and unchecked. When these conclusions become so solidified in the minds of their holders that even if they do finally bring them to the other party, they are unable to be challenged.

The other person can say "That is not true at all, here is what happened." But nothing can be done, because the lie has taken the place of the truth.

Mind reading feels harmless, because to a certain degree "jumping to conclusions" or "making assumptions" doesn't sound all that evil. We all naturally tend to think in these ways. But make no mistake: when we engage in these, we are condemning without a hearing. These things cause us to unknowingly believe and then spread very damaging false witness about others.

Just because a story makes sense in your mind doesn't mean it is true. In our marriages, friendships, and close relationships we should constantly do the work of checking conclusions and clarifying assumptions. If we don't, no one will like the outcome as unreality and division drive us apart.

SLANDER BY TWISTING WORDS

Consider another phrase meant to put skin on our breaking of the ninth commandment: twisting words. Picture yourself re-telling an event or conflict. Maybe you are hurt or angry. How objective are you, really, in the midst of powerful emotions and motivations? Is it possible you slant things in your favor, heighten the malevolence of your spouse or friend, without even realizing it?

> *"We don't even have to try. We do it naturally. We know how to retell a story so that we're the hero and others are the goat, where we emphasize only the really mean thing they said to us but say nothing about the hard and hurtful things we may have said. We're masters at passing along our interpretation of the events as if it were factual. Whether we realize it or not, especially when we're engaged in some sort of conflict, we intuitively know how to pass along information with a certain implied tone. We know how to leave out information and summarize long conversations in a way that makes us (or our side) look good and others (and their side) look bad. Don't think that "spin" is just what famous people do. We all spin."*

Kevin DeYoung, *The Ten Commandments*

We all spin. And spin is, whether we like it or not, participating in unreality. It's false witness to the situation, and it leaves wreckage in its path.

Nothing is exempt from its forest-fire like destruction—it comes for your friendships, heads straight for your church. It throws your marriage into disarray as it scatters shrapnel around the living room. The best of Satan's deceptions occur when you don't even realize things are crumbling around you and you walk away feeling entirely justified.

Jesus calls us out of this whirlwind of spin. He says to walk out into the light of reality (John 3:19-20). To deal with the log in your own eye before worrying about the speck in another's eye (Matthew 7:4-5). He has in mind healed and whole relationships where we confess our sins and suspect ourselves because we see ourselves as the worst sinner in the relationship (James 5:16, 1 Timothy 1:15). He calls us to tell the truth, because He is the truth, and the truth will set us free (John 14:6, John 8:32).

A PASTORAL WORD ON A CULTURAL WEAKNESS

If we can, let's get personal for a moment and dig down into our specific culture. Since 2007, our church has been meeting regularly in the Columbia area. From the beginning, our dream is that we would create a culture that rejects the shallowness found in much of current church culture and live out the vision for church family we see in the New Testament. That has happened in staggering ways that would require many pages of stories and many tears.

But as is common, the closer people get to one another, the more their sin hurts each other. And in a very inexact but educated guess, our pastors might say that there has been no more detrimental sin issue to the health of our community than the breaking of the ninth commandment that has been described here.

Gossip. Slander. Assumptions. Mind reading. Condemning without a hearing. False witness.

All of these have decimated relationships and trust. Torn apart LifeGroups. Caused untold damage to marriages and friendships. Threatened the health and vitality of our community.

On one level this is not a surprise. The Scriptures call us to a baseline default of putting the best construction on everything, as Luther says. To give the benefit of the doubt and be charitable of others. But our sin natures and culture team up to train us in the opposite: to be cynical, distrustful, jaded, hard-hearted. To put the worst construction on things.

We can't tell you how many pastoral conversations and meetings we've had over the years where we've had to say, "Well, that is the absolute worst way you could interpret that scenario, but there are other options." Part of that, like the story shared by the pastor above, has been directed at us in leadership.

That's no surprise, seeing that we pastor a young group of people raised in secularism that have historically high levels of distrust in authority of any kind. Another pastor from Greenville has go-to questions for this dynamic: *Is there any other way you could explain that? What if the opposite of what you think is actually true?*

But many times the negative lens is not directed at us, but at a LifeGroup. At another believer. At a spouse they are sitting on the couch with. It's just as destructive and pervasive there.

We have been trained to assume the worst. We do it without thinking, or even realizing it. And it causes unspeakable destruction, because it tears down everything it touches.

So...(family meeting style)...

Can we not?

Can we not assume the worst about one another?

Can we not mind read?

Can we not see scenarios through the most negative light possible?

Can we try to put the best construction on everything, to actually assume the best about one another?

Can we realize that sometimes someone else's "sin" is actually an unmet expectation we have that we haven't verbalized to them, so they don't know and haven't actually agreed to it?

Can we go to one another in radical honesty and check our assumptions, say: "Hey, I just realized I was thinking this, about you or this situation. Can you clarify that for me?"

Can we agree that if you have processed things with your therapist or a friend and have assumed things about others, but haven't gone directly to the person you have an issue with to confront, clarify or reconcile—that qualifies as gossip and is disobedient to Scripture?

Can we refuse to let the falsity of our tongues burn things to the ground around us?

Okay, good. (Family meeting over).

CRUCIFIED BY FALSE WITNESSES

As in all of the commandments, Christ stands as the only One who never succumbed to the temptation to lie. He never testified falsely, never gossipped, never slandered someone through mind reading or assumptions.

He never twisted His words to paint others in a negative light and He in a positive light. He never engaged in condemning without a hearing.

Never.

He told the truth in every single instance, no matter the cost to Himself.

So it is ironic that He who never lied was sentenced to die because of lies. He was led to the cross by false witnesses who said He was guilty of crimes He didn't commit.[125]

While we were not part of that particular crowd in Jerusalem, we are false witnesses.

All of us.

We did not physically lead Him to the cross, but nonetheless He went because of us who have shattered the ninth commandment in a myriad of ways, known and unknown.

Thank God that He went there—that He did not call down legions of angels who could have quickly righted such an unthinkable wrong.

Thank God that He allowed mere humans to excruciatingly execute His only Son—the source of reality itself.

Thank God that the Truth was killed, so we who lie could go free.

---

125 Kevin DeYoung, *The Ten Commandments.*

INTERLUDE 12
THE PERFECT SON &
THE DISCIPLINE OF GOD

"How kindly has God thwarted me in every instance where I sought to enslave myself."

Robert Murray M'Cheyne

In chapter 1 we noted that the Ten Commandments, in addition to the moral laws given to Israel specifically and God's people generally, are also a Father/son talk. God called the singular "you" of Israel out of slavery to live in His land and be His collective son, or daughter. They are rules for living in His house, under His authority, and they are unequivocally for our good.

They were designed to form Israel into the image of his Father. But in the immediate aftermath of Sinai, the Israelites show signs of being unable to hear their Father's voice and be conformed to sonship. The singular "he" of Israel speaks up with one voice to ask Yahweh to speak through Moses. Their hearts are too hardened to listen to their Father.[126]

This would continue to play out through the rest of the Old Testament in the many, many failures of God's people. Hearts continued to be hardened in rebellion, and people kept on doing whatever was right in their own eyes (Deuteronomy 12:8).

But Israel, though hard-hearted and rebellious, is not left hopeless.

"Yahweh will have a son who conforms to the Ten Words. The Father does have such a Son, the eternal Son who became Israel to be and do what Israel failed to be and do. The Ten Words are a character portrait of Jesus, the Son of God."

Peter Leithart, *The Ten Commandments*

126 Peter Leithart, *The Ten Commandments.*

Jesus showed up in first century Israel and turned so many heads precisely because He displayed perfect adherence to the Ten Commandments. They are, in a way, a prophecy that points directly to Him. The law has many uses—to show us our sin, our need for a savior, and be a guide—but "the first use of the law is christological."[127] The law shows us what Jesus would look like when He arrived.

And wow, was He beautiful.

He never once put another god before Yahweh, His Father. He did not bow down to created images of any kind—never tried to rule over what He was meant to bow to, never bowed to something He was designed to rule over. He never treated Yahweh or His name with less than the respect and reverence deserved. He perfectly observed the Sabbath, and in doing so became our Sabbath rest. He never committed a murderous act, nor had a murderous heart. Never committed adultery with his body or with His mind. He never stole through greed or through laziness, never participated in the unreality of lies, never coveted what did not belong to Him.

The Earth could hardly contain the radiance of a perfect Son taking back up all the dominion that Adam laid down and Israel couldn't pick up. Waves hushed at His words, fig trees withered at His touch, and the towering cycle of death itself was helpless against Him.

All the less-than-perfect sons and daughters marveled at the abnormalcy of a perfect Son, until He would not submit to their rival gods. Then rage ensued, and they had the perfect Son killed.

Possibly, during the inhumane suffering He immaculately endured, some began to see the light. The first son was gathered to God at the base of a mountain, the second Son was crucified on a hill. Thunder and thick darkness enveloped them both. As the perfect Son paid for the sins of the first son, a Roman soldier proclaimed the most likely explanation: "Truly this man was the son of God!" (Mark 15:39).

The perfect Son walked out of His grave three days later, instituting a new kingdom where sin and death no longer reigned. At Pentecost, God gathered imperfect sons and daughters and breathed His Holy Spirit upon them, writing not on tablets for the New Israel, but on human hearts (2 Corinthians 3:3). These Spirit-filled sons and daughters were

---

127 Ibid

unleashed into a life of spreading the gospel while growing ever more closely to resemble the perfect Son.

> *But when the fullness of time had come, God sent forth his Son, born of woman, born under the law, ₅ to redeem those who were under the law, so that we might receive adoption as sons. ₆ And because you are sons, God has sent the Spirit of his Son into our hearts, crying, "Abba! Father!" ₇ So you are no longer a slave, but a son, and if a son, then an heir through God.*

Galatians 4:4-7

The Israelites were slaves to Egypt and became sons on Sinai, Christians were slaves to sin and became sons through the grace of adoption. The gospel does not call us to simply marvel at the perfect Son in gratitude while we continue our disordered and deformed lives. It calls us to sonship.

THE DISCIPLINE OF GOD

The writer of Hebrews gives us a framework to put this process of learning to be God's child in: that of discipline.

> *Consider Him who endured from sinners such hostility against Himself, so that you may not grow weary or fainthearted. ₄ In your struggle against sin you have not yet resisted to the point of shedding your blood. ₅ And have you forgotten the exhortation that addresses you as sons?*
>
> *My son, do not regard lightly the discipline of the Lord, nor be weary when reproved by him.*
>
> *₆ For the Lord disciplines the one he loves, and chastises every son whom he receives."*
>
> *₇ It is for discipline that you have to endure. God is treating you as sons. For what son is there whom his father does not discipline? ₈ If you are left without discipline, in which all have participated, then you are illegitimate children and not sons.*

Hebrews 12:3-8

The perfect Son did not have an easy road Himself, enduring such agony in the Garden of Gethsemane that He sweat drops of blood. After acknowledging that we have not yet resisted sin to that level of distress, we are reminded of the shocking reality that God now calls us sons and daughters.

The Greek word for discipline is roughly "child-training"—the difficult and involved process a good parent goes through to get a sinful child to respect authority and become a good human that is beneficial for society. That's what God is doing for us, the writer says: treating us as sons. He's child-training us. Disciplining us.

This is not evidence of meanness or of spite, but in fact evidence of the opposite. It's evidence that we are actually sons and daughters. If we don't experience discipline, it means we are illegitimate children—not sons. The ancient world found it incomprehensible that a father could love his child and not punish him or her, because of the greater glory and responsibility that was to be theirs in time.[128] Illegitimate children did not have the same future glory, so the same effort was not made for them.

It is worth stopping to note that again, in our culture we do not have a high value for authority, so this concept can land a little uncomfortably. "Discipline" can feel harsh and undesirable in a culture so steeped in care/harm thought. We don't always see it in the frame presented here, and sometimes confuse the very important difference between hurt vs. harm. Biblically speaking, sometimes small hurts are necessary to avoid bigger hurts. As pastor Timothy Keller notes, "It's only through the little shipwrecks that we avoid the big one."

This concept of God's discipline would have been easier for the original hearers. We have trouble wrapping our minds around the discipline of God, not because of logic, but because of strong cultural forces. As one biblical scholar notes:

> *"A father who neglects to discipline a son is deficient in his capacity as father, and a son who escapes all discipline is losing out on his sonship. This is a principle which would not be recognized by all schools of thought in this modern age where permissiveness has such powerful influence. The authority of parents has been so eroded that discipline rarely if ever comes into play. It has generally ceased to be a part of sonship. It is small wonder that those brought up in such an atmosphere find genuine difficulty in understanding the discipline of God."*

> **Donald Guthrie, *Hebrews***

---

128 F.F. Bruce, *The Epistle to the Hebrews.*

But no matter our emotional feelings about the term, the logic is simply unavoidable: parents only put in the difficult work of raising and shaping the children that belong to them. They don't discipline the severely out-of-line kid at Target, they are glad they don't have to.

Discipline is proof of, and evidence of, love. Not the opposite.

The author goes on:

> *Besides this, we have had earthly fathers who disciplined us and we respected them. Shall we not much more be subject to the Father of spirits and live? 10 For they disciplined us for a short time as it seemed best to them, but he disciplines us **for our good**, that we may share his holiness.*

Hebrews 12:9-10

Did you catch that? He disciplines us *for our good*.

Are you sensing the theme through the entirety of Scripture? He is for our good. Always.

Even the painful process of discipline is "for our good, that we may share in his holiness." So we will grow to look more and more like the perfect Son, and experience the boundless joys that come with life in God's house. He continues:

> *For the moment all discipline seems painful rather than pleasant, but later it yields the peaceful fruit of righteousness to those who have been trained by it.*
>
> *12 Therefore lift your drooping hands and strengthen your weak knees, 13 and make straight paths for your feet, so that what is lame may not be put out of joint but rather be healed.*

Hebrews 12:11-13

Those of us who had parents who believed in "the rod" (to borrow language from Proverbs) and used it reasonably know this well. The pain endured was to ensure that when we grew up we would no longer lie, manipulate, bully, dominate authority, or fill-in-the-blank. So we would not grow up to do the much more damaging adult versions of kid sins. Because while a 7-year-old boy with a rebel's heart can only do so much damage to others, a 25-year-old man with the same heart can do unspeakable harm.

Small pains were meant to lead away from much bigger ones.

God is doing the same with us. His discipline of His sons and daughters is also painful rather than pleasant. Many times, this discipline is nothing more than the consequences of your sinful actions in the world. When you have an affair, pain and chaos follow. When you steal or lie, harsh consequences are often on the way. When a kid routinely disrespects his parents, he is set up for a difficult life. When you give way into addiction, climbing out of it will be extremely painful.

As pastor Matt Chandler says, 9 times out of 10, the punishment for sin is simply the consequences it brings. (Addiction leads to pain and life chaos, affairs can lead to divorce, etc.) Sin always has consequences. But there is also a category for God allowing you to experience extreme difficulty or pain for your spiritual growth.

This must be distinguished from suffering in general—not all forms of suffering are discipline, and that is very important to note. (Note: other people's aggressive sins against you would be an example of something that likely isn't God's intentional discipline of you). We don't have a perfect way to know what God is or is not using for discipline in our lives, and it may be a fool's errand to try to discern that during our life here. But this gives us the category.

God, at times, lets us or even leads us into things or seasons that are profoundly difficult. Things that are just downright painful—not pleasant in the slightest. And these particular instances are meant to yield the peaceful fruit of righteousness in us.

To make us look more like the perfect Son.

The passage ends with a picture of someone defeated by hardship or discipline. Maybe he or she doesn't understand what is happening. He has drooping hands, she has weak knees. With this framework, the writer calls us out of that defeatedness. "Lift your drooping hands...strengthen your weak knees," he says. "Make straight paths for your feet, so that what is lame may not be put out of joint but rather be healed."

The end goal of looking like the perfect Son allows us to get back on our feet through the pain, not letting it lame us permanently but moving through it to the healing and holiness on the other side. While it may not always feel like it to you, being formed into the image of Christ, biblically speaking—is a joy worth any pain you have to go through. Even, as Hebrews 11 points out, the potential of martyrdom.

Speaking on this passage, pastor Sinclair Ferguson drives the idea home:

"'My life is falling apart...I cannot understand what God is doing...' There is in a sense one simple answer to this question: He is treating you as a son. 'Oh,' you say, 'He wouldn't treat His son like that...His son wouldn't be bashed around like that...a real father with his son would make sure he did everything he could to protect him from sadness and pain and tears and challenges and difficulties'. No, says the writer—that would be a sign that the child wasn't legitimate. Think of God's only begotten Son, and His life, and how His heavenly Father loved him, and all that He had to endure...if I could just grasp this...'I am treating you as one of my children', so that the family likeness you bear will not primarily be the family likeness of the family in which you were born, but in the family likeness of the Lord Jesus Christ.

Is that the way you think about yourself, in every situation that causes pain? 'I'm just a little child, heavenly Father. I can hardly imagine what you are training me for. I understand there is an enormous distance to go, but this one thing I understand—I am Your child and you are training me for glory.' So hold onto me. Continue to be my Father....Yes, He's there, He's child-training you."[129]

Sinclair Ferguson

Children never fully understand what their parents are doing while they are children. They don't know exactly what is training and what is not, why certain things are so important, or what the purpose of some difficulties could possibly be. That's how it works. But Lord willing, when they are raised by good and faithful parents, they will be formed into a person who looks back and understands.

As Christians, we can be confident that the same is true for us. Through our meager understanding of things beyond our grasp, we can be certain that God is forming us into the image of the perfect Son, because that is the best thing that could ever happen to us.

He is for our good.

Always.

---

129 Father and Sons | SermonAudio https://www.sermonaudio.com/sermoninfo.asp?SID=6101374036

CHAPTER 13
YOU SHALL NOT COVET

SANCTITY LOYALTY

> You shall not covet your neighbor's house; you shall not covet
> your neighbor's wife, or his male servant, or his female servant,
> or his ox, or his donkey, or anything that is your neighbor's.

Exodus 20:17

Yahweh liberated his son Israel, and he wants his son to live in freedom—free from tyrannical gods, free from idols, free to rejoice, free from fear of violence, seduction, theft, rumor, and gossip. These freedoms are achieved, however, only if the souls of Israel are free, free from evil desires and fixed on true riches.

Peter Leithart, *The Ten Commandments*

COMING AFTER DESIRES

There is a way to read the tenth commandment almost as a nice, parting shot. Where in the midst of serious and weighty matters covered throughout (like murder and adultery), the list wraps up with some vague, flighty notion of "Try to be happy with what you have."

That would be a misread indeed. The last commandment digs deep—not concerned with actions, but with the desires underneath them. This opens up another world of complexity to consider.

We are not given a breezy conclusion, but one that pierces straight to the core. It is clear evidence that God is not simply after our behavior, but after our hearts. In order for Israel to truly be free under God's rule, their souls would have to be free.

WHAT IS COVETING?

First, it's not desire. Scripture affirms desires as good, such as the desire to marry, the desire for sex, the desire to save money for the future, the desire to have children. The Bible gives no guarantees that any particular desires will be fulfilled for a specific person, but certainly has a category for desires being healthy and good.

For simplicity's sake, we could say that coveting, then, is one of two things:

1. **Desiring the wrong thing.** Something that isn't yours, and never will be (your neighbor's wife, house, or possessions). This is more than acknowledgement of desirability or admiration, it's a wayward and obsessive desire to have what isn't and can't be yours.

2. **Desiring the right thing the wrong way.** Instead of waiting on God to possibly fulfill desires you have in ways that line up with His authority, you take off on your own and fulfill them outside of HIs design.

In Colossians 3, Paul says covetousness is idolatry. It is wanting and valuing something more highly than God—setting you up to choose and chase that thing over Him. This is played out in stories throughout the Bible.

In fact, the first sin was an act of coveting. Eve coveted the beauty, taste, and knowledge of the fruit, so she took something that wasn't hers. Cain coveted God's acceptance of his brother Abel, and then killed him. In Genesis 34, Shechem coveted Dinah and raped her, showing the despicable acts that can and do result from unhinged desire. (He and his people also paid a dear price for this unthinkable sin). David coveted Bathsheba, then forcefully took her and had her husband killed. In Joshua 7, Achan covets treasure that didn't belong to him, and steals it from Yahweh.[130]

These examples show the serious weight of coveting, and the destruction it brings. This is no mere advice, it is a life or death matter. James makes the connection clear:

> *You desire and do not have, so you murder. You covet and cannot obtain, so you fight and quarrel.*

> **James 4:2**

Coveting is the heart issue that leads us to break other commandments. It refuses joy in God and what He's given to chase idols, it causes us to murder, steal, and lie. It is a fountain from which evil pours forth.

---

130 Peter Leithart, *The Ten Commandments.*

A THEOLOGY OF DESIRE

Earlier in the book of James, we are given some clarity on the relationship of desire and sin.

> Blessed is the man who remains steadfast under trial, for when he has stood the test he will receive the crown of life, which God has promised to those who love him. ₁₃ Let no one say when he is tempted, "I am being tempted by God," for God cannot be tempted with evil, and he himself tempts no one. ₁₄ But each person is tempted when he is lured and enticed by his own desire. ₁₅ Then desire when it has conceived gives birth to sin, and sin when it is fully grown brings forth death.
>
> **James 1:12-15**

Here we see the immaculate purity of God: He tempts no one, because He can't be tempted with evil. Rather, each person is tempted when they are *lured and enticed by their own desire.*

So the desire itself isn't stated as sinful. Some desires can be sinful, but here there is no ruling on the sinfulness of the desire itself.

Then desire when it has conceived gives birth to sin. This is interesting language. What does it mean for something to be conceived? It has to be taken in, received, welcomed. So in the act of taking in a desire and feeding it, allowing it to stay and ruminating on what it would be like to meet it in a sinful way, that is where sin is birthed. And then, as the passage says, when sin is fully grown it brings forth death.

This means we are not called only to submit our bodies as a sacrifice to God, but our desires as well. He is to be Lord of both our outer behavior and our inward desires and thoughts. His sanctification of us goes all the way down into our wants.

OUR DESIRES ARE TO MATURE

James wraps up his teaching on desires and sin with the following summary:

> Do not be deceived, my beloved brothers. ₁₇ Every good gift and every perfect gift is from above, coming down from the Father of lights, with whom there is no variation or shadow due to change. ₁₈ Of his own will he brought us forth by the word of truth, that we should be a kind of firstfruits of his creatures.
>
> **James 1:16-18**

The problem is not that we desire, but that our desires are immature. We are bent to the core by our sin nature, and therefore don't want the right things. We are often deceived, even about what we want, and what we think it will provide for us.

This is behind the story of idolatry through the Scriptures. We turn and chase things we think will satisfy us, and they only bring ruin. As Peter Leithart says, "'Follow your heart' is paralyzing advice to someone whose eyes are dazzled by every passing beauty, whose vacuous soul is blown about by the most recent Tweet."[131]

Part of sonship is recognizing that every good and perfect gift is from above, as James says. Coming down from the radiant Father of lights, who never changes or disappoints. He brought us forth to know to become remade creatures who have learned to enjoy and want things that are good for us, having forsaken the wayward desires that only brought pain.

Our desires are to mature just as our behavior is to mature. Our hearts and wants follow our actions.

Is there any particular food, maybe an unhealthy snack or a fast food restaurant, that you used to enjoy but now find repulsive? That is the idea here—that new and better desires (for healthier or more high quality food) uproots and replaces old desires. The Bible doesn't teach us to demolish our desires, but rather to allow them to mature by the power of the Holy Spirit at work in us.[132]

So when we find in ourselves desires that are bending toward the wrong thing, or seeking to be fulfilled outside of God's design, we take those desires to God in submission. We ask Him to mature our desires. As the Father of lights, He teaches us through sonship to prefer and want the best gifts that come only from Him.

CAN DESIRES REALLY CHANGE?

The idea of maturing desires can be met with pushback, especially in our culture. We tend to see desires as immutable, or unchangeable. *The heart wants what it wants, right?* Our default position on desires is not that they are fluid, malleable, and subject to maturity—but that they are fixed.

---

131 Ibid
132 Ibid

So if you want something you always will, and if possible you should chase it.

Author Skye Jethani argues that our culture has taught us to think this way:

> "The idol of desire, and our consumer society that worships it has done a remarkable thing. They have convinced us that our desires are immutable and undeniable; that we are defined by longings and are powerless to change or resist them. With some desires this is true. I cannot deny my desire for oxygen—it is hardwired into my brain, but my craving for sugar is a physical and psychological desire that can be heightened or diminished. Our desire-worshipping culture wants us to believe that every desire is hardwired; that we are powerless victims of our appetites.
>
> The truth is, we have far more influence over many of our desires than we want to believe. We can choose to feed or starve them; to awaken or sedate them. When I remove sweets from my diet and eat more protein my craving for sugar diminishes. Likewise, I am more motivated to exercise when I'm part of a community committed to fitness. Learning to control appetites, delay gratification, and acquire new desires is precisely what allows children to mature into adults. We all possess this ability, we've just forgotten."

This vision is far more thoughtful and nuanced than the immature depiction given by our culture. We are not simply animals with appetites, born to hunt. Instead, we are image bearers holding the breath and design of God, with not a small degree of control over our desires. They can be fed or starved, awakened or sedated. They can grow in an immature, fleshly, animalistic direction, or they can grow in a redeemed, Spirit-filled, image bearer direction.

Our souls were made for weighty treasures that lighten us, but in our sin we constantly chase hollow treasures that shrivel and deaden our souls.[133] As C.S. Lewis says, we are far too easily pleased—like a child content to make mudpies when a vacation at the beach is offered instead.

Yet another dynamic of desire not often considered is the fact that they are both "caught and taught." We foolishly think that our desires are purely

---

133 Peter Leithart, *The Ten Commandments*

instinctual, when in reality culture and forces around us have a profound impact on what we do and do not desire. If asked why you desire a particular thing, you may respond with "I just do." It's usually far more complicated than that. Someone or something likely played a role in teaching you to desire that thing.

We are born coveting, and then trained to further covet from birth. We mimic the desires of others in ways we don't realize, co-opt them subconsciously—catch them as if they were contagious.[134]

In such a context, where our sin natures, our culture, Edward Bernays— and even Satan himself has played such a large role in shaping and molding our desires, we would be foolish to not want them to mature.

THE MORAL FOUNDATIONS OF DESIRE

An obvious connection can be drawn from the nature of desire to the moral foundation of sanctity. In Christ, we are called out of immature and debased desires to cultivate matured and sanctified desires. Notice the use of high/low language Paul uses for this in Colossians 3, and the link he makes to coveting:

> *If then you have been raised with Christ, seek the things that are above, where Christ is, seated at the right hand of God. ₂ Set your minds on things that are above, not on things that are on earth. ₃ For you have died, and your life is hidden with Christ in God. ₄ When Christ who is your life appears, then you also will appear with him in glory.*
>
> *₅ Put to death therefore what is earthly in you: sexual immorality, impurity, passion, evil desire, and covetousness, which is idolatry. ₆ On account of these the wrath of God is coming. ₇ In these you too once walked, when you were living in them. ₈ But now you must put them all away: anger, wrath, malice, slander, and obscene talk from your mouth. ₉ Do not lie to one another, seeing that you have put off the old self with its practices ₁₀ and have put on the new self, which is being renewed in knowledge after the image of its creator.*
>
> ***Colossians 3:1-10***

---

134 Ibid

We have been raised with Christ out of the muck of darkness and animalistic, evil desire. Now seated with Him, we are taught to desire things that are above—the holy, pure, and eternally worthwhile.

As the old self was fixed on Earth, the new self is to be fixed on glory. To be, literally, "renewed in knowledge," or matured, "after the image of its creator."

Note how many of the sins mentioned here are directly correlated to the second table of the Ten Commandments. Debased desires cause us to lie, lust, slander, become wrathful and impure. These form the "low," or base desires we are called out of through sonship. We are called to resist the contagion of evil desires found here on Earth, and cultivate the contagion of higher desires fit for an image bearer.

As always, this trade is for our joy and good, because only the Father of Lights gives every good and perfect gift (James 1:17).

Consider also the foundation of loyalty. God alone gives perfect gifts—He alone can be trusted to fulfill the desires He created. So what happens when we forsake the eternal pleasures of God's house and strike out like prodigal sons and daughters, looking for earthly consolations wherever we fancy them to be? Coveting breaks trust with God, because it says He isn't enough.

What He's given you isn't good enough.

What He's preparing you for, even through any difficulty or perceived lack, isn't enough.

You want something *else*.

Something *now*.

The wrong thing, or the right thing the wrong way.

Coveting is the opposite of contentment. Contentment says, "If I have God, I have all I need. I can trust Him with all of my desires." To borrow the language from chapter 11, contentment preaches that I don't need a product to meet some deeper desire, because a product *can't* meet a deep desire. Clothing *can't* give me an identity, a new car *can't* give me approval, cigarettes *can't* give me freedom—no matter what the ads say.

This is exactly the truth that Paul writes about from his jail cell in Philippians 4:

> *Not that I am speaking of being in need, for I have learned in whatever situation I am to be content.* 12 *I know how to be brought low, and I know how to abound. In any and every circumstance, I have learned the secret of facing plenty and hunger, abundance and need.*

Philippians 4:11-12

When you have a treasure as surpassing as Christ, other things just don't move the needle that much. Even good things, like not being in jail. In Christ, we are freed from needing other things to be content.

THE REVERSAL OF THE CURSE

The entire tragic drama of sin started with an act of coveting in the Garden. Adam and Eve, surrounded by a perfection unimaginable to us, fixed their eyes on the one thing that wasn't theirs to take. The forbidden fruit was appealing to the eyes and also to the heart, with the raised status they thought it would give them. *Control over good and evil? The ability to do as I say and please?*

The desire went unsubmitted, and birthed sin. Hands reached out to steal the coveted fruit, and death shortly followed.

So as God gathered the descendants of Adam and Eve at the base of His mountain, the last word was a warning not to follow in their first parents footsteps. It paints the picture that sons and daughters, when faced with the same predicament, will learn to do the opposite.

When tempted to desire the wrong thing, or the right thing the wrong way— when eyes light up with forbidden wonder and hearts race at the thought— God's children will say:

No.

They will turn away, back to the Garden's endless delight. Their hearts confirming: that is *not* for my good, because *my Father* is for my good.

But as we know, the law would not be enough to accomplish this and reverse the curse of Eden. We would need far more than instruction or even help—we would need a *rescue* of grace—a perfect stand-in who never once coveted what was not His to take. We would need the perfection of His life and His death, so we could be raised *with Him*—our evil desires included.

We would also need the supernatural indwelling and empowering of His Spirit, who comes to live inside of us to teach us how to live like we have been raised with Christ. Our eyes and hearts no longer fixed on the small and low treasures of this world, but trained on the high and weighty things.

On the distant country the Father has called us to—where all of our desires will be not only be met but overflowed, in the most perfect of ways.

CONCLUSION
WHEN YOUR SON ASKS YOU IN TIME TO COME

We started this journey with a story about a father and a son from ancient Israel, set in the sixth chapter of Deuteronomy.

Presumably, this father was eager to train his son in gratitude and obedience to God, because he knew what slavery was like

What it was like to work until your bones hurt. He had witnessed the cruelty of Egypt firsthand, and the desperation of seemingly unanswered cries for help.

Although those cries did not go unanswered after all, because a Father in heaven was listening, and He was far stronger than the rival god Pharoah. He stretched out His mighty hand and delivered His people, brought them to the base of Mount Sinai to be sons instead of slaves.

So this father was busy with the spiritual work of the Shema, the famous Hebrew call to worship.

> *"Hear, O Israel: The Lord our God, the Lord is one. ₅ You shall love the Lord your God with all your heart and with all your soul and with all your might. ₆ And these words that I command you today shall be on your heart. ₇ You shall teach them diligently to your children, and shall talk of them when you sit in your house, and when you walk by the way, and when you lie down, and when you rise. ₈ You shall bind them as a sign on your hand, and they shall be as frontlets between your eyes. ₉ You shall write them on the doorposts of your house and on your gates.*

Deuteronomy 6:4-9

This father was trying to point his son to the wisdom and work of Yahweh, the God who rescues with grace. He was teaching God's laws diligently to his children, anywhere and everywhere. While sitting, walking, going to bed and rising at the light of day.

So they would know, so they would flourish.

So they would, hopefully, *hear*.

So they would never go back to the back-breaking despair of slavery to harsh rulers with ruthless demands.

But kids, they always have questions, don't they? They see the efforts their parents make to teach them, and they ask the age-old question:

Why?

This response was not only anticipated, it was expected. The questions future generations would have about God's rules were deemed worthy of a gracious answer:

> *"When your son asks you in time to come, 'What is the meaning of the testimonies and the statutes and the rules that the Lord our God has commanded you?'* 21 *then you shall say to your son, 'We were Pharaoh's slaves in Egypt. And the Lord brought us out of Egypt with a mighty hand.* 22 *And the Lord showed signs and wonders, great and grievous, against Egypt and against Pharaoh and all his household, before our eyes.* 23 *And he brought us out from there, that he might bring us in and give us the land that he swore to give to our fathers.* 24 *And the Lord commanded us to do all these statutes, to fear the Lord our God,* **for our good always**, *that he might preserve us alive, as we are this day.* 25 *And it will be righteousness for us, if we are careful to do all this commandment before the Lord our God, as he has commanded us.'*

> **Deuteronomy 6:20-25**

Why does God give us these commandments and boundaries?

There is only one answer to that question, forever and always:

Because He is for our good.

For *your* good and *my* good and *his* good and *her* good.

That will never change, because it's been proven through rescue—first by a parting of the sea and then by the shedding of blood.

And as it turns out, both rescues were about sonship. The first turned slaves of Egypt into sons and daughters of Yahweh, the second adopted slaves to sin into the eternal family of God. Together they form the great story of how God reversed the curse of Eden, and vanquished the enemy of everything good and holy.

God has always been aiming for sons, for daughters, who trust Him. Who love Him. Who submit to Him. And therefore who are filled with the eternal delight that proceeds from Him alone.

He calls them to Himself, even still.

So...if you have a son or daughter who "asks you in time to come..."

Our churches have filled to the brim with little image bearers, delighted in by both us and God. The world they are growing up in is different than the one in which we did. Their world will be more solidly post-Christian than ours was, and they will have even more potential to be confused, perplexed by God and His intrusive rules.

They will ask questions, in time to come.

What is the meaning of this, they will say, although likely in different words.

Why does God ask this of me, of us, of them?

Why does He forbid what seems just fine, even good, to me?

What reason could He possibly have?

I don't understand...

And we will tell them, first and foremost, that God rescued us from the hand of Satan, sin, and eternal destruction. That He earned our ruthless trust with the blood of a perfect Son, proved once and for eternity that He is for our good, whether we understand it or not.

In time, we can also tell them that a culture and history-spanning God has more categories for morality than our culture does.

That certain things we don't understand are often explained when we zoom outside our fish bowl to see the multi-faceted wisdom of God.

That we've been redefining good and evil since the very beginning, and it hasn't worked out so well.

That you can judge God if you want to, but you are judging Him with capacity He gave you.

That freedom on our own terms has some benefits, but also some gruesome costs we won't want to pay.

That the "gospel" of secularism is in fact, no gospel at all.

That Emmaus has some worldly comforts, but they are paltry and sad compared to the resurrection joy of Jerusalem.

Lord willing, our children will listen.

Hear, and learn.

That God is for our good, always and always.

Until the far reaches of forever, where matured and truly free sons and daughters will still laugh and dance around His table.

Like they are just getting started.

WESTERN SECULAR LIBERALISM[135]

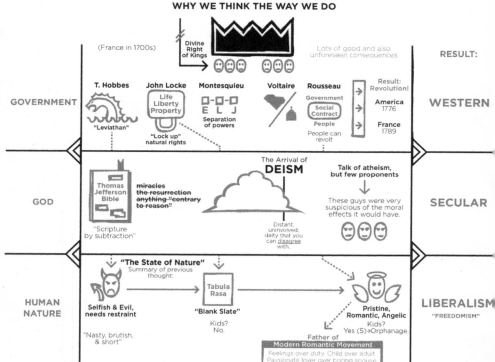

THE ENLIGHTENMENT
WHY WE THINK THE WAY WE DO

APPENDIX 1
WESTERN SECULAR LIBERALISM VIDEO TRANSCRIPT

It's hard to see the cultural water you swim in, so let me sum it up in 3 big, multifaceted terms: Western. Secular. Liberalism (and by "liberalism," I don't just mean the political left...more on that later). To explain what these terms mean, we'll look at 5 men who have profoundly shaped the way you think, even if you don't know who they are.

In 1700s Europe, there was a time period called the Enlightenment. Until this time in human history, the most common form of government, by far, was an absolute monarchy. There was a king over some people, the king would tell the people what to do, and the people would do it. Monarchies were backed by a widely held principle, The Divine Right of Kings, which argued that kings got their authority from God, therefore giving them the right to rule. For those in its wake, the end result of this period would cut the line running from heaven to Earth.

VIEW OF GOVERNMENT/AUTHORITY

There were many Enlightenment thinkers—we'll start with Thomas Hobbes. Hobbes, in some ways symbolizes ways of thinking that were defeated in the Enlightenment. He lived through the English Civil War where 400,000 people were killed, and saw many atrocities as a result of rebellion. He wrote a book called Leviathan (think, sea monster) that argued government is needed to restrain the worst impulses of man, and that left to our own devices, we might just kill each other. He believed that we should be thankful for the protection even imperfect governments provide, because their benefits are likely better than the alternative of chaos and constant war.

A man by the name of John Locke disagreed. He said that humans are born with what he called "natural rights." These rights were life, liberty and property. And that the government's job is to "lock" up those natural rights for its citizens. And if a government doesn't provide those personal protections for the individuals underneath it's authority, they have a right to rebel and form their own government.

Next was Montesquieu. He agreed with Locke and said, "But wait...what if that new government becomes corrupt itself, and uses its power to oppress people?" He thought there should be a separation of powers to keep each other in check: an Executive branch, a Legislative branch, and a Judicial branch.

Voltaire came along and argued strongly for the separation of church and state. Originally from France where there was a high degree of, um, cooperation between the state and the Catholic church, he visited Great Britain and praised their comparative toleration for different religions. He remarked how if a state had one religion it would get corrupted, if it had two they would kill each other, but if it had many everyone should get along nicely.

Lastly, Jean-Jacques Rousseau. Rousseau argued that there should be a "social contract" between the government and its people, and if the terms of that contract were violated the people could revolt and rip up the contract.

The result of these mens' writing was REVOLUTION. First, us. The American revolution came in 1776, and as Thomas Jefferson wrote the Declaration of Independence he channeled the ideas of these men, hoping his words would form an "expression of the American mind." The French Revolution followed shortly thereafter in 1789. All of this formed the foundation for Western democracy and Western individualism, as the focal point of society descended from the divine or a sovereign authority, to the encircled, "unalienable" rights of the individual.

VIEW OF GOD

The man who wrote the Declaration of Independence is famous for another literary reason—the Thomas Jefferson Bible. He formulated his own version of the Bible where he cut out the miracles, the resurrection, and anything he deemed "contrary to reason." His effort has been deemed "Scripture by subtraction," creating his own authority by removing anything he didn't agree with or like.

This was a direct result of Enlightenment teachings that elevated science and reason, producing doubt and skepticism about the supernatural and ultimately heralding the arrival of what we now call Deism. God exists, but he is distant, uninvolved, non-specific, and you ultimately have control over him. As fellow Enlightenment thinker Thomas Paine wrote, the deist relies solely on personal reason to guide his creed. There was talk of atheism at this time, but few were proponents of it, and many including Locke and Voltaire were very suspicious of the moral effects it would have on a society. The rise of a Deistic god you can disagree with, skepticism of God and his claim to authority over life, and doubt of the supernatural form the basis of a Secular culture.

VIEW OF HUMAN NATURE

The Enlightenment also had profound effects on the way we view human nature. Ironically, several of these men used the phrase "the state of nature" to describe what men would be like without outside influences, but they meant vastly different things by it. Thomas Hobbes summarized the previous cultural and historical thought as he believed that humans are selfish and have evil desires that need to be restrained. The prevailing thought was that nature had a profound impact on kids, that they were born with pre-programmed ideas about God, morality, and justice but were often unable to live up to those ideals because of brokenness inside them. His famous quote is that on our own life would be "nasty, brutish and short."

John Locke, again disagreed. He wrote that kids are what he called "tabula rasa," or a "blank slate." He argued that nurture and education makes them what they are, so if they are evil it's because someone taught them to be. He is the reason we are all terrified that we are going to do something to mess our kids up, and why we feel so much pressure to give our kids "good" childhoods. Thanks, John Locke. If you're wondering if he had kids, the answer is no. He didn't like them very much.

Rousseau took that line of thinking even further, arguing that humans are born with pristine, romantic, almost angelic natures, and that civilization and outside forces are what corrupts our nature. He wrote a book called "On Education," which is believed to be the most influential book on parenting and education in Western culture. Did he have kids? Yes, 5 of them. He left all 5 in an orphanage from birth...

Rousseau is considered the father of the modern Romantic movement, which as opposed to Classical ways of thinking, emphasizes feelings over duty, child over adult, and passionate lover over boring spouse (which, you might note, is pretty on-the-nose for how modern Americans tend to think).

He wrote a novel called "Julie" about a wealthy woman's love triangle between an exciting tutor and her boring husband. His contemporaries saw her love for the tutor as unwise and a passing fancy, but he painted it in a pristine, higher light. This paved the way for, well, almost any love story or movie you've ever seen.

All of these ideas about human nature paved the way for what we now call "liberalism"—an ideology that forms the foundation for democracy based on the ultimate idea that individuals should be "free" from tyrants, oppressors, and limits on their freedom.

In our American political framework it includes Democrats, who often prioritize freedom from any restraints on an individual's body, sexual expression, or gender, and Republicans who often prioritize freedom from restraints on our wallets, businesses, or nation. Both decry government overreaches on our freedom in different spheres.

But politics aside—"freedomism" also becomes an ethos where we believe centralized and inherently good-natured individuals should be able to throw off any outside restraint put on them—that individual rights are "unalienable," even by God, leading to an idolatry of freedom where any sort of limit on what you value feels like oppression.

In this mindset, any limit on your freedom can feel like suffering, and God is only useful if he can coexist with your true god of freedom. But if He won't, well...then He's the new King George. And we, like Thomas Jefferson, are tempted to cut out undesirable parts of Scripture to produce a god of our own making—a false god, maimed by razorblades, who submits to our declarations of autonomy and independence.

The spirit of our age can become a never-ending search for an oppressor. And no matter what you find your oppressor to be, the worldview of Western Secular Liberalism will wholeheartedly affirm your right to revolt against it.

APPENDIX 2
LIST OF COGNITIVE DISTORTIONS

There are many lists and descriptions of cognitive distortions found online. The following list is copied from the Appendix of *The Coddling of the American Mind*. It is one of the most succinct and helpful lists we found (with examples).

CATEGORIES OF DISTORTED AUTOMATIC THOUGHTS

MIND READING: You assume that you know what people think without having sufficient evidence of their thoughts. "He thinks I'm a loser."

FORTUNE-TELLING: You predict the future negatively: Things will get worse, or there is danger ahead. "I'll fail that exam," or "I won't get the job."

CATASTROPHIZING: You believe that what has happened or will happen will be so awful and unbearable that you won't be able to stand it. "It would be terrible if I failed."

LABELING: You assign global negative traits to yourself and others. "I'm undesirable," or "He's a rotten person."

DISCOUNTING POSITIVES: You claim that the positive things you or others do are trivial. "That's what wives are supposed to do—so it doesn't count when she's nice to me," or "Those successes were easy, so they don't matter."

NEGATIVE FILTERING: You focus almost exclusively on the negatives and seldom notice the positives. "Look at all of the people who don't like me."

OVERGENERALIZING: You perceive a global pattern of negatives on the basis of a single incident. "This generally happens to me. I seem to fail at a lot of things."

DICHOTOMOUS THINKING: You view events or people in all-or-nothing terms. "I get rejected by everyone," or "It was a complete waste of time."

SHOULDS: You interpret events in terms of how things should be, rather than simply focusing on what is. "I should do well. If I don't, then I'm a failure."

PERSONALIZING: You attribute a disproportionate amount of the blame to yourself for negative events, and you fail to see that certain events are also caused by others. "The marriage ended because I failed."

BLAMING: You focus on the other person as the source of your negative feelings, and you refuse to take responsibility for changing yourself. "She's to blame for the way I feel now," or "My parents caused all my problems."

UNFAIR COMPARISONS: You interpret events in terms of standards that are unrealistic—for example, you focus primarily on others who do better than you and find yourself inferior in the comparison. "She's more successful than I am," or "Others did better than I did on the test."

REGRET ORIENTATION: You focus on the idea that you could have done better in the past, rather than on what you can do better now. "I could have had a better job if I had tried," or "I shouldn't have said that."

WHAT IF?: You keep asking a series of questions about "what if" something happens, and you fail to be satisfied with any of the answers. "Yeah, but what if I get anxious?" or "What if I can't catch my breath?"

EMOTIONAL REASONING: You let your feelings guide your interpretation of reality. "I feel depressed; therefore, my marriage is not working out."

INABILITY TO DISCONFIRM: You reject any evidence or arguments that might contradict your negative thoughts. For example, when you have the thought "I'm unlovable," you reject as irrelevant any evidence that people like you. Consequently, your thought cannot be refuted. "That's not the real issue. There are deeper problems. There are other factors."

JUDGMENT FOCUS: You view yourself, others, and events in terms of evaluations as good–bad or superior–inferior, rather than simply describing, accepting, or understanding. You are continually measuring yourself and others according to arbitrary standards, and finding that you and others fall short. You are focused on the judgments of others as well as your own judgments of yourself. "I didn't perform well in college," or "If I take up tennis, I won't do well," or "Look how successful she is. I'm not successful."[136]

136 Greg Lukianoff & Jonathan Haidt. *The Coddling of the American Mind: How Good Intentions and Bad Ideas Are Setting Up a Generation for Failure* (pp. 277-278).

CPSIA information can be obtained
at www.ICGtesting.com
Printed in the USA
JSHW031232130621
15866JS00002B/4